BORN
FOR
THIS

ALSO BY BEBE WINANS

The Whitney I Knew (with Timothy Willard)

BORN
FOR
THIS

MY STORY IN MUSIC

BEBE WINANS

New York   Nashville

FaithWords
Hachette Book Group
1290 Avenue of the Americas, New York, NY 10104
faithwords.com
twitter.com/faithwords

First Edition: October 2019

FaithWords is a division of Hachette Book Group, Inc. The FaithWords name and logo are trademarks of Hachette Book Group, Inc.

The publisher is not responsible for websites (or their content) that are not owned by the publisher.

"The Question Is" by Marvin Winans. Copyright © 1981 Bud John Songs (ASCAP) Crouch Music Corp. (ASCAP) (adm. at CapitolCMGPublishing.com). International copyright secured. All rights reserved. Used by permission.

"Born For This" by Benjamin Winans. © 1998 EMI Blackwood Music Inc. All rights administered by Sony/ATV Music Publishing LLC, 424 Church Street, Suite 1200, Nashville, TN 37219. All rights reserved. Used by permission.

Unless otherwise noted, Scripture quotations are from the Holy Bible, New International Version®, NIV®. Copyright © 1973, 1978, 1984, 2011 by Biblica, Inc.™ Used by permission of Zondervan. All rights reserved worldwide. www.zondervan.com The "NIV" and "New International Version" are trademarks registered in the United States Patent and Trademark Office by Biblica, Inc.™

Scripture quotations marked (ESV) are from the ESV® Bible (The Holy Bible, English Standard Version®), copyright © 2001 by Crossway, a publishing ministry of Good News Publishers. Used by permission. All rights reserved.

Library of Congress Cataloging-in-Publication Data
Names: Winans, BeBe, author.
Title: Born for this : my story in music / BeBe Winans.
Description: First edition. | Nashville : Faith Words, [2019] | Includes bibliographical references.
Identifiers: LCCN 2019007476| ISBN 9781546009894 (hardcover) | ISBN 9781549175923 (audio download) | ISBN 9781546009887 (ebook)
Subjects: LCSH: Winans, BeBe. | Gospel musicians—United States—Biography. | Rhythm and blues musicians—United States—Biography. | Singers—United States—Biography. | Christian biography.
Classification: LCC ML420.W5648 A3 2019 | DDC 782.25/4092 [B] —dc23
LC record available at https://lccn.loc.gov/2019007476

ISBNs: 978-1-5460-0989-4 (hardcover), 978-1-5460-0988-7 (ebook)

Printed in the United States of America

LSC-C

1   3   5   7   9   10   8   6   4   2

To my father, David Winans Sr., for the many lessons you taught us—through words and actions—about how to love and care for all. And even after you departed from earth, your words still guide me.

To my big brother, Ronald. Not a day goes by that I don't think of you fondly, sometimes bringing me to tears, which quickly turn to a smile . . . and then an outburst of laughter. I miss you, I love you, and I can't wait to see you again.

CONTENTS

CONTENTS

BORN
FOR
THIS

CHAPTER ONE

WHO AM I?

I will sing to the LORD all my life;
I will sing praise to my God as long as I live.

—Psalm 104:33

I've been so many people in my life: a kid, a son, a boy, a brother, a friend, a grocery store clerk, a choir singer, a husband, a father, a Grammy winner, a Grammy loser, a producer, an entertainer. As I've followed the path set before me, I've experienced a world tailor-made for me, just like yours is tailor-made for you. And each experience has taught me just that little bit more I needed to get by, to overcome, to find success, to mend fences, to realize a dream.

My father used to tell me, "Know who you are before

you walk out that front door, because if you don't, the world will decide for you, and you'll lose your way."

Boy, was he right. I've had plenty of opportunities to lose my way in this world. But my father's words always rang in my ears like church bells. It's one thing to remember those words of warning, but quite another to live by them. I've come to realize that it's the living day by day that tells you who you are. We unravel throughout this life, learning from our mistakes and victories. We become who we are by the decisions we make and the people we meet and the friends we keep. This is true of every person on the planet. I'm no different from anyone else. I'm flesh and blood with feelings and dreams, with concerns and questions—questions that found some answers along the way and questions that linger in my brain like a suspended D chord. Although disappointed and knocked down at times, I always found strength to rise again. How?

Well, it was a combination of things. But it all begins with my family. I know I'm blessed to come from a family of ten children and two parents who were strict but loved us unconditionally. I don't take that for granted, ever. It all started with Mom and Dad and the strong faith they instilled in all of us when we were kids.

As I spoke with my mom and siblings while writing this book, my life opened up before me in a profound way. Mom reminded me of how our current family formed;

unorthodox and unapologetically filled with music. My brother Marvin helped me see into our family's past. He reminded me that though my roots still remain in Detroit, they also reach further back to another time, another place. And it was in revisiting and reviving some of the places in my memory that I found clarity for my life now.

These memories and discoveries reminded me that life can be difficult and wonderful, beautiful and ugly, brilliant and messy. But it's precisely those times when everything gets cloudy and our confidence grows thin and our belief in where we're going falls into question that we reach back to the roots that shaped us. Because you and I are more than our most recent failure or our greatest achievement. We are parts of history unfolding. You and I live in the "to be continued" moments that our parents, and their parents, never dreamed about. You and I are like notes in a chord, giving the song rise, giving the melody symmetry with our sad and glorious moments of life.

My story is like yours. I've fallen. But I rise again, over and over. And like you, I've experienced times of happiness. We're born for both. And I've found that wonderful moments make life worth living and living well. And inevitably it's those moments we rise that we look back on and say, "Wow, look what I learned there. Look how that changed me."

I was born to write songs. Yes, most days. I was born to

be a father. Yes, and two is enough, which is funny to me coming from a close-knit family of ten crazy kids.

But life has shown me that our sweet spots grow from the bitter moments. This truth tells me now that I was born to be ridiculed. I was born to be lied about. I was born to be mocked. I was born to be hated. I was born to endure emotional pain. And best of all, I was born to be misunderstood, and who wants that? These moments made me just as much as all the bright moments the world sees.

God reaches out for us. And we must reach back. Without God as my source, I am nothing. And I am who I am today only because of Him. When I searched for meaning in life, He gave me purpose. When I stand tall in this world, I do so only because He stands next to me. He showed me how my failures and pains add to life's journey. And it is only with them that I was able to arrive at a place of wholeness and joy. I've only now begun to live out my purpose.

All this—the pain, the brilliance, the everydayness of it all? I was born for this.

A "born for this" mind-set can conquer a "this world is killing me" mind-set. It's a change of heart, a change of perspective. It gives you permission to look at everything that comes your way with the confidence that says, "Yes, come on now. Here we go. This obstacle is mine, and I'm ready for it."

When you recognize that you're equipped for whatever life throws at you, your anxiety subsides. It doesn't necessarily make everything perfect, but when your mind is set upon something in a new and fresh way, it can be the difference between living in fear and defeat and living in joy.

Come with me as I share my journey, and let's learn together. Let's remember the past and look toward the future. Let's think through the hard times, and lament if we have to, and rejoice in what is to come.

CHAPTER TWO

THE LONG JOURNEY HOME

The ache for home lives in all of us, the safe place
where we can go as we are and not be questioned.
—Maya Angelou

As it turns out, home is more than a place. Home is
the people you love. Through all my wanderings, through
Detroit, Pineville, and Nashville, I never fully figured this
out. I had a home in the hearts of my family even if I
never found another place where I felt as though I really
belonged.

It took a tragedy to teach me this lesson.

LOSING MY LIFE

Seems like only yesterday I stood in the crowd with my

sister CeCe, watching our brothers perform, wishing it were me. And eventually it was. First it was CeCe and me, then me. A revolving door of music made, music sung, music performed, music loved.

Time passed on our careers.

CeCe and I produced albums, together and solo; we toured; we raised our families; we said goodbye to our dear friend Whitney; and time continued its march. But the learning in life doesn't disappear with the flower of youth. The lessons continue to mount. So much has changed.

But what hasn't changed is our beginning. That always remains a forever memory that I continue to draw from. Families grow, and sure enough, the Winans family grew big. But in the growing and learning and living and singing, we experienced loss.

And it was deep.

CeCe and I were in different cities when she and I, along with the rest of our family, received a dire phone call from our brother Marvin, informing us that Ronald was back in the hospital. "You need to drop whatever you are doing and come home to Detroit right away," he said. "I don't think this time will result in the same outcome as the emergency did nine years ago."

Nine years earlier the entire family received a similar call, and we all converged on Detroit. It was for Ronald then too. He'd had a heart attack. Our family witnessed the power of God while in the waiting room, as doctors tried to save Ronald's life. The doctors lost him on the operating table, but it wasn't Ronald's time back then, in 1997. God performed a miracle and gave us back the gift of Ronald's life that night.

But there was no denying the urgency in Marvin's voice. I feared the worst. "Ronald is in the hospital again," he explained. "Something about complications—he's retaining fluid. You need to come soon. And, BeBe, this isn't just for a visit. We aren't going to tell Ronald to get well this time. You need to get here knowing that this time it's to see Ronald off. He's going home. The doctor said that they're going to keep him on the machines until the entire family gets here to say goodbye."

Caught off guard, I answered my brother's plea. "Yes, Marvin. I understand. I'll be right there," I said. I rushed to the hospital, as did our entire family. When I arrived, I asked for Ronald's room. A nurse directed me down a few different hallways. I ran, wanting to be in Ronald's presence for every moment he had left. I expected to be the last one to the room. But when I arrived at his room I noticed that Mom was sitting with Marvin in a different room, away from the tragedy my family was about to witness.

I remember walking into that room and seeing my mom sitting calmly with Marvin, upright. Surprisingly, there was no trail of tears to wipe away from her face. After a few moments, the nurse came in the room and beckoned us to come, encouraging us to go and say goodbye. But

Mom wouldn't go, so Marvin and I left her sitting there in silence and quickly walked into Ronald's room to say goodbye to our dear brother.

But how do you say goodbye to your life?

And he was my life in so many ways. Yes, I had five other brothers whom I loved deeply as well, but Ronald was the glue and the bridge to all the facets of life for me growing up—I mean *everything*: films, food, music, God, and just living in general. He introduced me to all those things in a way that opened my eyes to them and helped me experience them in wonderful and beautiful ways.

And now I'm told to say goodbye to all that? All that he gave me? I would rather trade places and ask God to take me. He meant too much to me, to be absent from this earth for the rest of my days here.

Marvin and I went into the room together. Everyone else was already there, our brood of siblings, gathered in a circle around him. I will never forget the scene. I can still see Marvin in front of me, walking straight toward Ronald's bed and laying his body on top of Ronald's like a blanket, covering him in tears and trying to tell Ronald how much he meant to him, and how he was going to miss him, and how we would never forget him. Even now, tears swell in my eyes as I'm reliving that moment while writing this. Losing those you love hurts. The initial pain leaves its mark, and like any scar, it flares up unexpected and pronounced.

After Marvin, I followed suit, and while rivers started running down my face, I tried to tell Ronald what he already knew.

He knew I loved him with all my heart. He knew life would be really difficult for me without him by my side cheering me on, saying, "Little boy, you can do it," standing there at the finish line with a big grin and the dimple on the right side of his cheek, saying, "I told you so." And now I was saying goodbye to all that security and unconditional love that flowed from his heart straight to mine for most of my life.

Mom wouldn't come in because she didn't want to see her son with all those wires and tubes in him—no, she wanted to remember him without all those things. And Mom was right. There was something wrong about seeing my brother like this. He was only alive because of these machines, because of the countless people bustling around the room. This wasn't the right place for a song, even a sad one. The other Winanses in the room held one another and prayed; all, except Mom.

Then Mom sent word that she was going to come in and say goodbye. But she requested the nurses take all the tubes and wires out of Ronald because she wanted to remember her second-born son for the rest of her life without signs of distress, lying there in peace.

But even though Mom requested this, the nurses were not in agreement simply because they knew that if they did this, Ronald would, right away, take his last breath. And they wanted my mom to see him before he did. So, we went back out and told Mom what the nurses said. But she insisted, requesting that the nurses follow her instructions and rid him of all the attachments before she came in. So, reluctantly, they did. They removed all the tubes and wires. And every single person in that room watched as Ronald's heartbeat remained the same, and his eyes stayed wide open. He kept breathing on his own, and we waited for my mom to enter the room, and we waited, and we waited.

It felt like hours before she came in. I'm not sure how long it was. She finally entered the room. It had to be the most beautiful love scene ever witnessed. My mother walked over to Ronald, kissed him on his forehead, and placed her head on his chest. Then she took her hands and held his face softly and said to him, "It's OK, baby. It's OK. I will always carry you in my heart. It's OK."

And then her son, my brother Ronald, closed his eyes and left us.

It was as if Ronald was waiting to see and get permission from his mother to leave. And why not? All our lives, if my brothers or sisters wanted to do or go anywhere, we had to have permission from our parents. That was part of the rules in the Winans household. And this was a big ask, to go to a place of no return. But she accepted the facts, and permission was granted.

Dad gathered us together, and we cried as we prayed.

I can't even remember a word of the prayer.

All I wanted at that moment was to bolt out of that hospital. And I did after we said "Amen."

Ronald is gone. That's all I could say to myself.

And now, all these years later, I still feel the same way. After twelve-plus years without him, not a one of those 365 days has gone by without my thinking about him.

My friend Byron Cage picked me up from the hospital and drove me over to see my best friend, Margaret Bell. I desperately wanted Margaret to help me understand how God allowed this to happen.

On the way over to Margaret's house, with Byron breaking the speed limits, these words just kept bouncing around in my head: *Ronald is gone.* Just a few weeks earlier, he had been comforting me in my sadness and pointing the way forward.

We finally arrived at Margaret's house. And as she opened the door and came running out to comfort me, I remember opening the car door and falling to the ground, saying, "He's gone, Margaret. Ronald's gone."

She held me and said, "I know, BeBe. I know, my love. I know."

CHAPTER THREE

WHO DO YOU SEE?

Be yourself; everyone else is already taken.

—Oscar Wilde

Present day.

What is that? It's now, but it's also a collection of all the past days and experiences. Now, it's over twelve years since Ronald's passing. And he's still in my thoughts. When I sing. When I do my laundry. When I talk with Mom. Present day. And I'm still singing. I'm still walking down this path of music and performing. I'm older, hopefully wiser, and still growing, still learning. And I'm reflecting on life as it strikes my memories at odd moments, reminding me of my homeward journey.

A STORY OF PERFORMANCE

When I looked out of the sound booth, I saw the engineer, a couple of close friends, and lunch being delivered. That day I had driven up to the studio, through typical Nashville midmorning traffic, and settled in for a half-day session. I had to lay some new vocals on a song I'd already tracked months earlier.

But, as these things go in the music business, I had an idea and wanted to add something special to it—a few guest performers, a surprise for my listeners. Their tight harmonies and soulful delivery—mmm, mmm, I couldn't wait to get their vocals dumped into the existing track and record some of my own fresh tidbits.

When I arrived at Blackbird Studio in Nashville, the engineer, Jeff Balding, who's been responsible for not only the sound of all my solo records but also the sounds of the records with me and CeCe, had everything cued up, ready for me to begin.

But I had to listen to the tracks again with the additional vocals, the special surprise. And it was tasty. These cats were *singers*. And they were just kids. Their passion for music drew me in. I could feel it in their performance. They tucked themselves behind the notes. They surprised the listener at just the right time. And they delivered the good stuff, the payoff, at the perfect time. That's what I heard growing up. When my parents or siblings heard good singing, they'd say, "Now So-and-so, they're a *sanger*."

Now the tricky part. Stepping into the booth and laying some new ad-libs while also producing myself. No small task. I like to argue with myself. But I usually win.

And so, it begins.

The tracks light up in my ears, bright and rich and full.

I close my eyes, and I don't think. I just listen, and then I let the passion of the song move me.

It's all about performance. And I don't mean I'm in there putting on a performance. Anyone can perform in front of a crowd. But it takes something out of you when you really perform a song, while no one is watching or listening. But you better believe someone will be listening, years, even decades, later. And that performance you give in that moment, that lean in, that guttural you leave on the track, that's what the unseen audience will hear. That's a performance.

A performance is more than how you sing in front of people. A performance *means* something. You know when someone is performing to entertain and when someone is performing "the song."

I think most people can detect this difference between the entertainer and the real performer. They just don't know they're detecting it. When you listen to a master performer, you're listening to more than a song. You are actually stepping into the song and are transported by the performance. It's a balance of raw talent and polish, of extemporaneous ad-lib and what's written down on the paper somewhere.

Sometimes these master performances are so nuanced, it's hard to tell. You can have two phenomenal singers perform the same song. And both might make you cry. But there will be something that separates one from the other. This level of performing rises above the mere "I'm going to entertain you here for five minutes with this song I like to sing." The nuanced performance of seasoned singers can transcend the music that carries the song.

Both performers might be able to flawlessly sing the song. But one performance will touch something inside you—maybe a place that you didn't know the music could reach. But it's that special performer who not only feels the song, they become the song. They interpret the song from some deep place in their heart and soul. And that interpretation is what you hear. You don't feel like you're listening to just a song; you're listening to this amazing singer perform their very soul.

In such a performance, a story unfolds. It's not one you read or hear narrated. It's one you sense in the way the person carries each note, or slides in and out of their breaks, or restrains themselves, holding out the glut of their passion until it is appropriate.

And maybe it isn't appropriate at all. Maybe the song calls for a constant line of restraint. Maybe the passion of the song never comes in the much-anticipated glut of emotion. Maybe it comes in the final note of restraint, more spoken than sung. Sometimes the most beautiful, the most passionate, of things come to us in the quiet of an unforgettable note whispered on the ribbons of the microphone, fading back in the mix.

THE CADENCE OF BECOMING ME

I like to eat breakfast at Cracker Barrel. When I'm in town, it's my place to go after my early-morning workout. How early? Four thirty in the morning early. Years ago, I wanted to change my body—I wanted to lose all the weight I'd put on over the years of not taking care of myself. I got a trainer, and he helped me do it. He created a workout regime for me.

"If you follow this regime and stay disciplined, BeBe, you'll lose the weight. But you won't even know it because you'll be gaining muscle."

"Sign me up."

I do my best work in the morning, so I made my mornings about getting healthy, getting fit. It was a brutal process. Looking for shortcuts to a healthier life, to losing weight? I've got some news for you. There are no short-cuts. Only hard work. Sacrifice. Hours alone in the gym on the stationary bike or on the treadmill.

But it's not all bad.

I've formed relationships with a few people from my gym. We've become good friends. We keep one another accountable. You're less likely to skip a morning workout if you have a friend ask, "Hey, you didn't show up for the run this morning. What happened?"

But it's the feeling of getting healthy that's most addicting. You hack away at your body with blows of exercise and weight training. You don't skimp. You do it right. You use the right form. And you show up. Day after dreary day. I like to say my favorite time of day is when I'm done with my workout. It's true. I don't like doing it. I get it done and move on.

You may wonder how I can like feeling healthy but also eat at Cracker Barrel. When you work as hard as I do on the weights, you'll get it. I sit in the same area, so I can get the same server. I like the routine of it all. I like the simple things like getting up, getting the workout done, getting some breakfast. It's my every day. Even when I'm out of town, I get it done, one way or the other.

The gym. Cracker Barrel. Short nap in the morning. More work. Then the studio. My day unfolds like it always does.

And here I stand, tired, my arms sore from the workout, eyes burning a bit because I went to bed too late the night before. My days haven't always started this way. I'm aware of where I stand. And I remember what it took to get me here. And through it all, I'm still excited about the music, the process of making it, of getting it done and moving on to the next thing. And it's this awareness of who I am and where I've come from that gives me confidence to sing on.

THE RHYTHM THAT SHAPES ME

I like to sing in the car.

I hum and sing gibberish words to tunes I make up in my mind.

Thank God for the iPhone.

I sing or hum into the voice memo app and log them into my phone's memory. I have voice notes from six years ago. I have song ideas from creative sessions prompted by weird dreams that woke me up in the middle of the night, and because I couldn't go back to sleep, I composed with hums and made-up words. Those same gibberish tunes, those odd, obscure midnight melodies, they return to me, eventually. And it's always when I least expect it.

It's like I'm Elijah sitting out in the wilderness be-cause God told me to—although God would never tell me that because He knows the wilderness and I do not mix; it's only a metaphor—while the ravens bring me my food. Those tunes are my food, provided for me by God Himself. And they don't always make sense, and I don't always know what to do with them. So

I tuck them away for a time to come. And it always does come.

A songwriter's work is never done. It's perpetual. It wakes you up and says, "Time to work. Write me down so you don't forget." And you must obey, or you'll lose it. A singer's life is the rhythm life of musings and tinkering, of discipline and hard work. What I love most about the music in my life is its ability to continually shape me. I am not a kid anymore, listening to my brothers sing. But in a lot of ways I am still that kid—singing from the shadows of voices that shaped me.

I sing while I drive. I record while I drive. Why? Because the songs ask me to. Because, whether the public hears it or not, I'm a singer. And I know that because the songs tell me so.

LOOKING INTO GLASS

It's already time for lunch, and I've only just listened and made mental notes to myself and fiddled around with ideas. Oh, I've been singing. But not performing—not yet. I'm remembering; the structure, the words, the cadence, the gaps begging for some passion. But when you're in the studio, time can warp somehow, and suddenly the day is done and all you've accomplished is not much at all. These two hours evaporated in my mind.

We all dive into J. Alexander's—fish tacos, salads, a few

burgers—and talk about Gospel music and the Detroit scene from years ago. I dish on a few good stories I remember from growing up and hop back into the sound booth. It's time to roll up my sleeves and get some things down.

I slip on the headphones. The tracks play. And I'm feeling good. I'm hearing so much now. When I look out of the sound booth, I see Jeff the engineer, a couple of close friends, and the remnants of lunch being eaten and tossed. Some scroll their phones; others chat.

But I also see my reflection in the floor-to-ceiling glass rectangle separating me and Jeff. And there I see my white beard and my camouflage trucker hat resting loosely on my head. I see my eyes staring back at me and then:

I see the smile carving up into my cheeks.

I see a singer, yes.

But also, my mother's son. My dad's young boy. How time flies. Seems only yesterday I was playing with my cousins in the alleyway between our old church on 2135 Mack Avenue, Zion Congregational Church of God in Christ, and the old Baptist church. Today, I can stand in between the churches, stretch out my arms, and nearly touch both buildings. But as kids, we thought that alley was enormous. Time flies, yes, but it also morphs your perspective.

But that boy now stands as a man, still pushing through, still pursuing what I love, still trying to bring the message we like to call the "Good News" to people who have never heard it before and to the hearts of those who have heard it but need inspiration for another day.

That's what drives me. That's why I stand here in this studio, staring into this glass. I see the boy, the singer, but there's someone else in that stare. Hidden behind the ballcap grin and my father's eyes, I see a preacher.

CHAPTER FOUR

PREACHER MAN

A good name is to be chosen rather than great riches,
and favor is better than silver or gold.

—Proverbs 22:1 (ESV)

Who am I?

"Excuse me, sir, but I think you look a little bit like Mr. BeBe Winans."

"Yes, sir," I reply, extending my hand to the gentleman on the park bench. "And how are you today, sir?"

"I'll shake your hand, if that's all right."

"Of course."

We shake hands. He grabs my arm at the elbow and smiles. "A pleasure, Mr. BeBe."

That's who I am. Mr. BeBe. Or Benjamin, as my brothers and sisters call me. Although they call me BeBe as well.

Benjamin Winans. That's the name on my driver's license. But what's in a name? Quite a lot, these days. Your name is your brand, some say. But I'm not Nike or Starbucks; I'm not an organization that needs to form some kind of identity in order for people to buy what it's selling. I'm a human being. And this particular human being believes that my name is a way to identify the person God created me to be. My identity as a man, a friend, a father, is first found in Christ Jesus. No branding needed, thank you very much.

And yet my name is more than a simple identifier. God takes names seriously. He liked to rename people in the Bible. He changed Abram's name to Abraham. The name "Abram" meant "high father." But the name "Abraham" meant "father of many nations." And that's what God intended for Abraham—to be the father of many nations. God said that His descendants would outnumber the stars. So, in God's naming economy, a name signified a new identity. He did the same thing in the New Testament to Simon. He changed his name to Peter, which meant "rock." And He said, "Upon this rock, I will build my church." Names matter to God. When I think of my name, I think of my purpose and I think of my family.

I didn't think much of my name when I was younger. I

was just plain old Benjamin. And Winans wasn't anything special to me. It was just my last name. I didn't realize the importance of a name until I was much older. In fact, I'm still learning about my name, Winans. Once I was sitting with my nephew at lunch. He and I were eating lunch with my mother—his grandmother—Mom Winans. It came up that Mom had written a book years earlier. My nephew couldn't believe it.

"Grandma, you wrote a book?"

Then he discovered she played basketball.

"You played basketball?"

Then he found out she was nominated for a Grammy.

"Grandma, who are you? You were nominated for a Grammy?"

A friend was sitting with us, and he piped up and said, "Better learn about your grandmother, son. And about your own name, Winans."

It's true, though. When you're young, you really don't know anything about who you are, let alone the legacy of your name. And this word "legacy"—it is not reserved for successful people or families with long bloodlines or the rich and famous. We all leave a legacy—every person, no matter their station in life. It doesn't matter who you are or where you come from or to what religion you ascribe or the color of your skin; every person lives a life, and so every person leaves a trail of that life behind them. That's a legacy. I wish the younger generations would take pride in their personal legacy. I want them to understand that their legacy is about more than just their own life; it's about how their life touches others; it's about family; it's about what you leave behind for your family and your friends.

But I didn't know any of this when I was a kid. What I knew about my name came to me from my immediate surroundings, which was my siblings and Mom and Dad. It wasn't until later on in my life, when I became a young man, that I discovered that I wasn't born a Winans. And it was one of those things I discovered over time by observing our family.

"Now wait a second," I thought to myself. "Why do we have three sets of grandparents?" It wasn't one of those things people talked about in the church. No one said, "Now listen, my young little BeBe: your real grandparents had your dad out of wedlock." Oh no. God forbid the adults tell us the truth up front. They made us dig for it.

WHO I WAS

Now, I'm no historian, but I do know my family, thanks to the memories of my mother and my siblings. And as I walk you through my history, I'll lean on their knowledge and experiences to help spark my own.

The beginning is a very good place for me to start, but that's not everyone's story. My childhood, by every account, was a blessing. I was fortunate to have two parents in the household: a loving mother, Delores Amelia Glenn, who was born in Delray, Michigan—that's southwest Detroit, down river—and a hard-working, stern, but loving father, David Glenn, who was born in Detroit. Later in life people called him Pops, but for most of his life his close friends and elders called him Skippy. We called him Daddy, if we wanted to keep our teeth.

Early in his childhood, one of the ladies in his church nicknamed him Skippy when he was just a baby, and it stuck. My father was strict and funny at the same time. You may think the last name is wrong, but let it be known I was born a Glenn, not a Winans.

Laura Glenn gave birth to my father in 1934 at Parkside Hospital in Detroit. But there's more to the story than just Dad being born.

Laura was sixteen when she had my dad. Dad's father, Carvin Winans, was much older than Laura. Carvin denied that the baby was his. Maybe because the baby was born out of wedlock, who knows. This denial caused Laura to endure a good bit of pain and embarrassment. When asked who the father was, she replied, "Carvin Winans is the father."

But Carvin would not admit it. Laura, however, did not change her story. She stuck to it.

"You'll see, when the baby gets born," she said.

Carvin's father, I.W. Winans, told Carvin that he would

have no more children because he'd curse himself by denying that Dad was his child. And the scary thing is, Carvin never had any more children after Dad.

So the child, my father, took on Glenn, his mother's last name. Laura struggled with the reality that she'd have to bring up young David on her own. But Clare Glenn and David Glenn Sr., who were Dad's grandparents on his mother's side, reassured Laura.

"Don't worry about the child," they said. "He will be taken care of. We will help you raise him."

THE HANDSOME TROUBLEMAKER

Dad grew up mostly in the company of women after Carvin refused to accept that the baby was his. Laura and Clare took on most of the responsibilities of raising Dad.

It was widely known that when Dad was a little boy, he liked to act like his grandfather I.W. Winans, whom most referred to as Elder Winans. Elder Winans was a preacher at the Mack Avenue Church of God in Christ. And apparently, so was Dad. At least he acted like one.

One of Dad's cousins says their grandmother kept Dad in church when he was young. Which might explain his acting like a preacher. So, to play a joke once, they built a podium out of orange crates. And Skippy, well, Dad, stood up on the podium and preached, with his cousins and little friends acting as his "hallelujah section." Dad did his best to preach just like Elder Winans preached. Dad was also known as one of those boys always getting into some kind of trouble. (Dad never mentioned that much growing up. Can't let the kids know you were a troublemaker growing up—oh, Lord no.)

As Dad got older, he turned into a handsome man. And that's not only me saying so—that's what *he'd* tell you if he were here. He knew he had it going on. He'd probably tell you that he was always handsome—that it didn't just come upon him when he became a teenager. I guess that's what gave him some of the charm that everyone loved about him.

And as he was her only child, his mother used to spoil him with good clothes so that he always looked sharp. And the ladies took notice. He always looked good during his high school years.

It was in his teen years that Dad met my mom, Delores.

THE LADIES' MAN

Mom and Dad started singing and playing the piano when they were very young. They first met in the Lucylle Lemon Gospel Chorus in 1950; Mom was about thirteen years old, and Dad was fifteen. Dad joined when his mother, Laura, did. She brought Dad along because she didn't want to leave Dad home alone. My mom played piano for the group. She was young, eleven or twelve, when she first joined. She ended up playing and singing for over ten years with the chorus.

They toured nationally, so there was some cache to that. People knew them across the country. But not like in Detroit. In Detroit, the chorus were revered. People called Lucylle the "Doll of Gospel Music." It was an outlet for young singers and musicians to work on their craft. It was a symbol of opportunity, a pathway to the fulfillment of a young person's dreams.

But don't let the word "Gospel" in the name fool you. Not everyone was "saved" in the chorus, as Dad once put it. Many of the performers traveled and sang the Gospel songs because they just wanted to sing. Anyone could join the Lemon Gospel Chorus. It was a community choir, so it didn't matter what church you attended, or didn't attend; you could sing if you wanted to.

Dad remembers that one church did not invite them back because someone in the chorus was seen smoking a cigarette on one of their breaks. That was a big no-no in most churches during that time.

At one point during their time together in the Lemon Gospel Chorus, Mom says Dad was sweet on her and wanted to date her. Mom was a tough one. She told Dad he had to win her over. She knew that Dad was a ladies' man, so she made him work to win her heart.

Being in the choir was like a ladies' playground for Dad. He'd "go with" two or three girls at a time, as Mom recalls. And they knew he was dating all of them because they'd get together and talk about it. But Dad would tell you that he wasn't saved back then. He was just part of the choir, singing and enjoying the company of the ladies. I suppose in his eyes, they were better off getting a piece of him than none at all.

When it came to Mom and Dad eventually getting married, Dad remembers that he had "another choice." So how did he decide which girl to marry? He relied on his mom to give him guidance on the issue. And his mom told him that Delores, my mom, would be the best wife for him. He listened to his mom. Mom and Dad dated for three years and married in 1953. She was seventeen and he was nineteen! Remember that number—seventeen—for later on when someone else wants to get married young.

Naturally, when Dad married Mom, she became a Glenn and the first seven children she birthed were Glenns. I was the seventh son of the clan of ten. Seven boys, then three girls after me. The first girl was Priscilla Marie Winans, better known as CeCe. At the beginning, we were the Glenn family.

Dad left the Lemon Gospel Chorus for the very important reason that he couldn't see himself wearing a robe. He left and started his own group, a quartet called the Nobelaires. In one of their first shows Dad recalls their opening song was "Somebody Knows When I Am Tempted." And yet even though Dad was singing about being tempted, he still hadn't fully given his life to Christ. But that was about to change.

SPRAWLED OUT IN THE SPIRIT

One day, standing in the Parkside projects on the northeast side of Detroit, Dad felt the spirit of God move him. He'd tell you he still wasn't saved, but he felt God tell him that he needed to attend his grandfather's church. His grandfather was I.W. Winans, the bishop of Mack Avenue Church of God in Christ.

Dad recalls that it wasn't long after he experienced that feeling that someone told him there was going to be a meeting at the Mack Avenue church. A lady preacher was speaking, and it was widely rumored that she had the power of God in her life. Dad wanted to see what it was all about. So he attended the meeting, and when there was an invitation to come forward, Dad got out of his pew, went down the aisle, and stood in line.

"I didn't know what hit me," he says. "One minute I was standing there in the line, and the next minute, after the holy sister had laid hands on me, I was sprawled out on the floor."

Dad experienced the power of God profoundly that night. And things changed almost immediately in his heart. After that experience, he lost interest in the Nobelaires.

"I just wanted to be where the saints of God was testifying and glorifying God," he said.

It was after that experience that Dad began regularly attending his grandfather's church. I.W. Winans became Dad's pastor. Now, don't forget. At this point, Dad is still named David Glenn.

Dad's desire to be like the other singers, the other quartets in the area, disappeared. That competitive nature that so defined the music culture back then in the Detroit of his youth? Dad no longer wanted it. He only desired to be in church, to be experiencing God in powerful ways, and he attributed that to the guidance of I.W. Winans.

Stepping out of the popular music environment of the area was a countercultural thing for Dad to do. The guys in the quartet all attended church, and yet their lives did not necessarily reflect a changed lifestyle. But Dad insisted that he wanted to attend his grandfather's church—a holiness church. And when you attended a holiness church, there was no smoking, or drinking, or running the streets; there was no gambling. You didn't lead one life on the street and then another at church. It was wholesale transformation. So Dad left the Nobelaires and accepted Christ as his savior.

SKIPPY'S CHOIR

After Dad left his group, he decided to start a choir. And it's funny to me to hear some of the testimonies of some of the people who sang in it. Mostly because I'm not surprised one bit by their stories.

They described Dad as very demanding. Check!

Better than anyone else. Check.

Could do whatever he wanted. Check.

That was my dad. He was demanding, and he was good, and he wasn't shy about his gift. He was forceful because he was a force himself. And he'd get the best out of you by demanding the most from you.

They never rehearsed in the church but always at one of the choir members' home, at least early on. I love how Dad described how that early choir performed: "I didn't get up in front and direct, like choir directors do with their choirs today. No. Our choir was a family. We sang, prayed, ate together, and sang together."

Dad described their music community in the choir as a spiritually organic group. That choir did everything together, even fasted together. Fellowship defined their meetings and even their life outside of meetings.

"That kind of fellowship only comes from the love of God," Dad would say. "And it's a blessed thing."

And from that kind of love and togetherness came a glorious sound, according to my dad. I believe him.

And it wasn't only Dad getting involved and leading the music. He and Mom worked at it together. Dad led the song while Mom played the piano. And the group sang in the Spirit.

Dad was fond of this saying by his pastor, I.W. Winans: "You can't lead the Spirit of God; you've got to be led by the Spirit of God."

To put it simply, Dad just led the group up onstage and he'd start them singing, but that was it. They just sang. But it was singing in the Spirit of God—that's a different kind of singing, one you can't fabricate. It must come from the fellowship of the saints.

BECOMING A WINANS

It was during those days when Dad was leading the choir that his mom, Laura, fell away from the church. But he and my mom, and those first handful of children, had remained in the church and under the leadership of I.W. Winans. I.W. grew attached to Dad's seven sons. And he began to consider the fact that there were no Winans grandsons. Irvin Winans, Carvin's brother, had a girl, and after Dad was born, Carvin didn't have any more children.

On December 16, 1963, I.W. approached his son Carvin to ask him to see if my dad would change his name from Glenn to Winans. Surprisingly, Carvin made the request to my dad on behalf of I.W., in order to assure that his name would continue after he died. I was one year old at the time.

But Carvin failed to convince my dad to change his name. It was left to I.W. to do the convincing. Dad's relationship with Carvin Winans was strained due to the fact that Carvin hadn't been in his life much, so it wasn't a surprise that he failed. But Dad's relationship with I.W. was solid, and he convinced my dad to change his name to Winans. He even said he'd pay for all the children to have their names legally changed.

But Dad needed to talk with his mother, Laura, and with my mom about it. He needed to give it some thought. Mom was happy to do it, and Laura seemed to think it was fine. So Skippy and Delores changed our family's name from Glenn to Winans.

And yet even though Mom was happy to do it, and Dad, who never held a grudge, agreed to do it, I can't imagine how that must have made my grandmother Laura feel. And what about Laura's parents? They helped Laura raise Dad. Laura's mother, Clare, basically raised my dad until he was seven years old, when she died.

I spoke with my cousin Gwen about it to see if she could shed any light on the Glenns' true feelings. Gwen was Laura's niece. Gwen and my father were thick as thieves because they grew up together, so when my father passed, as much as we worried about my mother, we also worried about Gwen because of how close they were. And though Gwen didn't live in the area at the time, she told me that Laura had, indeed, been upset about the whole thing and that the Glenns as a family felt the sting of the situation as a kind of betrayal.

She reminded me that Laura had been only sixteen when

she became pregnant, and at that time in our culture, that carried a lot of shame. And she was stuck not only with the shame of being pregnant out of wedlock but also saddled with caring for her son on her own. It was a God-send that Clare and her husband were there to help her raise my dad.

The Glenns, as I discovered, viewed I.W.'s actions as an affront to them and their efforts to care for Dad. They saw it as I.W. simply wanting to secure the Winans name because, as my mom liked to say, "I.W. loved him some Skippy." To the Glenns, it was offensive for Carvin, who early on had always denied the child was his, to suddenly be given a brood of seven young boys to carry on the family name. He did nothing to deserve it. In fact, he'd done the complete opposite.

It wasn't as if it was one discussion with my dad either, and I think that's how I initially thought it happened. But the Glenns claimed that the Winanses talked Dad into it, they convinced him with sly arguments—things like, "David, you're living a lie because you're really a Winans." All because they wanted grandsons.

There are always two sides to every story. And the story of the Glenns and the Winanses proves that to me. I've never thought about the pain or shame that Laura must have endured until recently. I've never thought about how it must have felt to raise a child, who assumed your name because the father refused to claim his own son, and then have that very child cast off your name in favor of his "real" name, until now. They are painful thoughts.

But at the time, my dad was a grown man and he could make his own decision, and everyone knew and everyone respected that, though clearly not everyone agreed with it.

I suppose Dad could have felt betrayed by his father, Carvin. And maybe he would have had those feelings when he was younger. But Dad recalls that when I.W. approached him, he felt no ill will toward Carvin. He didn't hold a grudge even though no one would fault him for doing so. Dad believed that the most important legacy to leave in this world was the legacy of forgiveness. Dad believed that God blessed his act of forgiveness by blessing the name Winans.

"It is quite remarkable when I think about our family being an entire family of singers," he'd say. And it's now more than just our immediate family—the blessing of song and singing now extends to three generations. Could it be that the blessing of God extended to all the children, and the children's children, and on and on, just because Dad didn't hold a grudge? I can't say for certain, but I don't doubt it. God, I've discovered, is a God of blessing, of keeping His word, of letting His favor fall on whole families.

My perspective is not my dad's. I did not live through all the things he lived through. And it's fair to say his

Detroit was not my Detroit. I grew up in a much different environment than he did. Though I know the story of being born a Glenn, I've known myself to be a Winans since as long as I can remember. I can only imagine how hard it must have been to realize that your father denied you when you were a baby. And I can only imagine the kind of grace that has to exist in a person's heart to not hold a grudge over that. And that's a humbling thought.

THE MESSAGE OF THE MUSIC

Dad not only loved Gospel music, he loved the message. It came from his heart. Anyone who ever saw my dad perform live knows he put everything he had into his performances. If Dad was singing, you'd better hold on. And it wasn't all show—it was passion. And like Mom, he was a man of many talents. He also played the saxophone and the clarinet in the traveling chorus.

But once us kids came along, Dad quit singing out in groups. He didn't sing professionally again for another thirty years. Dad did what he had to do in order to support our family. And he had to. When it was all said and done there were ten of us siblings: David Jr., Ronald, Carvin and Marvin (they're fraternal twins), Michael, Daniel, and me—Benjamin. Then the girls showed up. First Priscilla Marie—though you know her as CeCe—followed by Angelique Lynette and Debra Renee. Our parents had their hands full.

Dad worked hard. And he worked all kinds of jobs. From a taxi driver to a car salesman to working at the Dodge plant in the early 1960s. He began preaching in 1969, though he would tell you he heard the call to preach before that but flatly ignored it.

Mom and Dad had their own dreams. But sometimes your dreams have to take a back seat to the reality of life. And life doesn't care if it shatters your dreams. It just keeps moving. You have to adapt and continue, or you'll find yourself strapped down by your own disappointment. And Mom wasn't going to let disappointment settle in. That kind of disappointment would have spelled trouble for her marriage and her family. Besides, there were other things in life that were worthwhile. She knew and believed in the value of music and in the value of work, and the two are not mutually exclusive. She and Dad drilled that into our hearts. We've all inherited it.

We all inherit values and characteristics from our parents. But some things in life you discover; they aren't inherited or instilled. I consider the Winans name a wonderful blessing from God, as Dad did. Names are important.

They carry with them the legacy associated with the many lives intertwined in that name.

But the Winans name didn't just end with the saga of my dad's past with Carvin and I.W. That's only one glimpse in time of a name that goes back much further than I realized.

CHAPTER FIVE

MY WHITE-ISH ROOTS

"Before I formed you in the womb I knew you."

—Jeremiah 1:5 (ESV)

I was fifteen years old.

Mom and Dad took most of us kids and some friends out to dinner after church. I'm not sure how they pulled that off as much as they did, because when the Winanses went out to dinner, it was a caravan of people. As we enjoyed our dinner one night, three white people approached our table. Now, at this point my family was somewhat known in certain circles in Detroit. So it wasn't altogether uncommon for us to be approached when we were out and about.

The three whites introduced themselves to Dad and

said, "I thought you might find it interesting that our last name is Winans too."

Dad looked surprised, and rightly so. Winans was not a popular name.

"Really!" Dad replied. "C'mon. Show me your license," he said with a playful grin.

The gentleman pulled out his license and showed Dad.

"Well, I'll be! I guess y'all were our slave owners!"

Cue the awkward pause in the very brief conversation.

Dad possessed the uncanny ability to say whatever was on his mind, and he really didn't care about the consequences. The man looked surprised but laughed awkwardly along with Dad.

To Dad's credit, he was right, at least from our limited perspective, to be skeptical. The only Winans any of us knew were, well...they were not white.

Years later, and when I say years, I mean several decades later, I was attending an event in Arizona. The white doorman at the hotel where I was staying pointed to his name tag as I walked in: Ray Winans.

"What? Really?"

I felt like my dad.

But sure enough, he showed me his license: Ray Winans. We chatted briefly and exchanged numbers, and then I went about my day.

Apparently, I didn't know all there was to know about the Winans name. And this intrigued me. I suppose if you really think about it, we're all related if you take the generations back far enough. But I had never met a white Winans.

If you want to really understand the Winans name, I discovered that you need to get to know my great-grandfather I.W. Winans and the church he founded, Zion Congregational Church of God in Christ, located in what is now the historic district in Detroit, Michigan, at 2135 Mack Avenue. I've always known who he was because of the connection to my father.

But there's a special history there that runs deep and dark, a reminder that while history can shape us, it's our dreams that define us.

THE MYSTERY OF THE PAST

As I reflected more on my past, I decided to visit home and talk with friends and family about growing up in Detroit. I flew from Nashville to Detroit to talk to my mom and to see old friends and to talk to my older brother Marvin. Marvin now pastors Perfecting Church in Detroit. I attended the service and visited with him afterward in his church office.

On his wall hung an old black-and-white photograph of

our great-grandfather I.W. Winans, or Bishop Winans, as we called him. I noticed the picture, half whispering the name "Bishop Winans."

"Ah yes," said Marvin, "good ol' I.W. God told him to come to Detroit. 'God sent me here,' is what he said."

"From where? I forget the whole story."

"He was part of the Great Migration, BeBe.[1] At least I think so—it makes sense given the year he left and the supposed time the migration began. They say the Great Migration began in 1915 and continued all the way until 1970. I.W. moved from Mississippi to Detroit in 1916, and three years later he founded the church you and I grew up in. Hard to believe nearly all of the African American folks lived in the South before 1910."

"Sure is," I said.

The influx of African Americans in Detroit in the early twentieth century is well documented. If you know anything about Detroit, you know that it has a rich ethnic history. This was on display with the forming of the well-known Black Bottom area, where people of all ethnicities settled.

"I.W. moved his family from Centreville, Mississippi, in order to start a church."

"In 1916? What was their life like before they came here?"

"Well, I can only imagine. But recently I did some digging on my own and discovered quite a bit of new information about our family you might find interesting."

It's hard to imagine what life was like one hundred years ago in our country. You hear stories on the news or watch a documentary or read a book, but all that frames the past in an almost unreal light. It's too easy to place my own perspective and context on a time that was completely different than ours is today. I mean, think about it. We didn't even have the first airplane until 1903, and that was only an experiment. Now, I use planes like folks back then used the train. I don't even give it a second thought. Our technology today makes our experience in life so different; our conveniences today were mere dreams a century ago—or not even thought of yet. But technology and convenience aside, what about the realities of being a black man in the South at the end of the nineteenth century? Many of us have stories about our experiences in the South, and I currently live in the South, but the South in the twenty-first century is nothing like it was in 1886. And still nothing like it was in 1916. So I wanted to hear more of what Marvin had dug up.

"Go on," I said.

"Here's what we know about I.W. Winans, as far as I can tell. He was born in Mississippi in 1875 to Antonio Winans. I could not find the name of his mother. When I.W. was born, his father was a sharecropper—that's when one family leases land from the landowner, and the landowner gets a share of the crops as payment for letting them work the land. I.W. was born after the Civil War, so naturally I was curious as to their 'situation' with regard to the slave culture of that time."

"Did you find out anything more about that?" I knew my brother had taken a trip down to Mississippi to dig around, but I didn't know what he actually discovered.

"I did. Remember, I drove down to Mississippi and visited with the folks at Millsaps College?"

"Yes, I remember."

"Well, I did that because there seemed to be a connection between Antonio Winans and this other Winans fella named William Winans. Before I get to William, all I could uncover about Antonio was that he was born in Chicot County, Arkansas, in 1838 and died in Wilkinson, Mississippi. Now today, Wilkinson is an actual community in Mississippi, but it's also a county. The county was founded in 1802 by European settlers who wanted to set up cotton plantations along the Mississippi River. The largest town in Wilkinson is Centreville.

"But, BeBe, here's the most interesting part: I couldn't find a record of the names of Antonio's parents. 'Names' end with Antonio; after him, it's just numbers. So I have no idea how or why he was born in Arkansas, but eventually, and somehow, he was brought to Wilkinson, Mississippi. My only guess is that he was either taken there by slave traders or that his parents took him to Mississippi. We just don't know.

"But remember the other Winans I mentioned earlier? His name was William Winans. And, BeBe, he was white."

"Excuse me? Maybe I should call Ray or get in touch with those fine folks from years ago we met at that restaurant with Dad and Mom and let them know that Dad was right!"

I was laughing and also surprised and a bit taken aback, having come face-to-face with this potential reality.

"Right, I know. I can't say for sure that there's a connection, but it seems likely given the times and the culture of the Mississippi Territory in the early nineteenth century. William Winans was born in Chestnut Ridge in the Pennsylvania Alleghenies in 1788. His father, Creighton Winans, was a cobbler, and his mom, Susana Hopkins, was a weaver. They later moved to Ohio when William was still very young. He spent most of his adult life in the Natchez Trace in the Mississippi Territory. He moved down there on December 4, 1810. Mississippi only became an official state in 1817.

"The Natchez Trace was not a great area. I read online that it was mostly known as a trail that was forged by deer and bison and was made into the Columbian High-way. But it was so rugged, the conditions so awful and remote, that it became known as the Devil's Backbone. William actually traveled this exact route on horseback as he traveled from Ohio to the Centreville area. It took him twenty-seven days to travel it."[2]

I had no idea about any of this, and it was still fresh on Marvin's mind—I could tell he was excited about it. It was like listening to someone talk about a treasure hunt, and all the details made the hunt that much more exciting and interesting.

"So why did William travel down to the Natchez Trace area if it was so brutal and gross?" I asked.

"Because he'd committed his life to God and wanted to be an itinerant preacher for the Methodist Church."

"So he was a preacher."

"He was, BeBe. He traveled hundreds and hundreds of miles on horseback—he became a circuit preacher. He was ordained by Francis Asbury, the great Englishman circuit rider who played a role in the spread of Christianity on the American frontier. William, like Asbury—and apparently this was something a lot of Methodist preachers did, going all the way back to Charles Wesley—kept a journal of his travels. I was able to look through some of his journals and letters at Millsaps College. It's fascinating stuff.

"Early in his life he was 'friendly' with the ladies; I read how he enjoyed spirited women and was enamored with Rhoda Gibson for some time."

"Yep, that sounds like a preacher," I said, laughing.

"He started riding his circuit, the Claiborne Circuit, on New Year's Day 1811. I can't imagine riding a horse for ministry, let alone riding it in those conditions. He had to contend with rivers, creeks, swamps, and navigate the ferries that operated on the Big and Little Bayou Pierre Rivers, as well as the Big Black River."[3]

It's hard to imagine a time like that. Marvin told me that the place William Winans lived was so remote that differences in skin color or class didn't matter because people were all just trying to survive. The people of the Natchez country were united simply because of the harsh conditions. Calamity unites.[4]

"Eventually," Marvin continued, "William married Martha duBose, and they started a life together on a small plot of land that had eight fields, which was given to them by Martha's mother. William built a small one-room house with a loft. Sadly, he built it with the help of two slaves who apparently came with the property. He and Martha called the house 'Rural Retreat.'[5] William's health forced him out of the circuit-riding ministry, so his mother-in-law suggested he serve as overseer of her property. The documents say that Martha's mom was especially harsh with her discipline of the slaves, but that William was compassionate and did not act like an overlord.[6]

"It's interesting, because though William worked for his mother-in-law and managed the property along with her seven slaves, he was not 'for slavery' as an institution as we might think of it. He didn't think, however, that the abolitionists provided a reasonable solution to slavery. Just freeing the slaves, he thought, would bring even more divisiveness and chaos to society. He wanted to work to return the slaves to their homeland. To him, that seemed the best solution. And yet, he 'owned' slaves himself. This was apparently a popular view among many in the South.[7]

"As I was going through the list of items in the William Winans archive, I found a 'bill of sale for slave' from 1859, and a 'receipt of bequest of female negro minor' from 1833.[8] A receipt of bequest means that the personal property was given through a will. So this earlier one might have been a slave left to him by Martha's mother—I don't really know. The point is, I guess, that William owned slaves but was not too keen on enforcing the institution of slavery itself as a cultural norm."

"So what does all this mean?"

"It means that our name is a slave name. And that it's possible our four-time great-grandfather was a white man."

CHAPTER SIX

MY FOUNDATION AND THE AIR OF HOPE

"Therefore, everyone who hears these words of mine and puts them into practice is like a wise man who built his house on the rock."

—Matthew 7:24

I stood there looking at that faded relic of a photograph—the one of I.W. hanging in Marvin's office, and it reminded me of my youth. Marvin showed me another faded black-and-white picture of all the congregants standing in front of the church, along the street, up and down the cement stairs that led to the top level where the sanctuary was. An old battered sign now hangs above the front door and reads, ZION CONGREGATIONAL CHURCH OF GOD IN CHRIST. We grew up running the halls of that church

I.W. founded there on 2135 Mack Avenue, two streets west of Chene. He started his ministry in Detroit when he migrated from Mississippi in 1916.

You can still find the tall and narrow brick building today. Services are still held there. My memories of that church simmer up from boyhood. And you know how it is when you're little; everything seems so big and grand then. The alleyway between Mack and the Baptist church that is right next door is only about six feet wide. Now I can stand in the center of the alley, stretch out my arms, and nearly touch both outside walls of the churches. But I remember that alley being as long as a football field and wide enough for us to play games and create whole worlds in our pretend universe. It was huge, then.

I can remember sitting in the worn wooden pews listening to I.W. and trying to be "good" so I didn't get in trouble after the service. The ceiling vaulted high, past the balcony, making the sanctuary room feel grand. I always wanted to sit up in the balcony. Today, the vaulted ceiling doesn't exist. It's been closed off, and a low ceiling now hangs, smashing the room into a shallow and cramped-feeling gathering place. The same pulpit still stands. And many of the wall hangings remain. When last I visited, it did not feel as alive as it did when I was a kid.

As I walked the halls of the old building, I could almost smell lunch cooking down in the basement room where the kitchen was, as if the smell was baked into the concrete walls. That's right: church included lunch. I remember how my siblings and cousins and I couldn't wait to run down the steps and dive into lunch. The only thing we were thinking by the end of the message was, "Hurry up and close the Word, Pastor, so we can get downstairs to that chicken." Because that's all we could smell by the end of the message: fried chicken and rice and cabbage—soul food—rising up from the basement.

Downstairs, along with the kitchen, was "small church." We kids did the Sunshine Band down in small church. Small church even had its own instruments, which included a piano and drum set. I remember singing "I Will Make You Fishers of Men" in small church.

But what I'm describing is only a building. And though the building still holds a nostalgic place in my heart, it's what we did in that building that shaped me: *worship.*

THE FRANTIC SCREAMS OF WORSHIP

Our home was nurtured under the wings of the church. And when I say "church," I mean a foot-stompin', hand-clappin', roof-raisin' Pentecostal church. I know, it's hard to know what all the names of churches mean nowadays. Just picture in your mind a service that began with really no start time. Pastor started church when the Holy Ghost arrived. And we all know the Holy Ghost doesn't get up until around 10:30 a.m. on a Sunday morning. And he's not ready to go home until, oh, you know, around 10:30 p.m. Church for us, growing up, was an all-day affair. Remember, we ate our meals there.

But when the Holy Spirit did show up, oh boy, you better watch out.

The worship time—the singing time—in church was our time to find out where our hearts were. We didn't know that then; we were just kids. But going to church was our time to discover what shape our souls were in. At Mack, the worship service was chaotic: people fighting for the song, dueling for the lead. You'll find more order in services today, especially at Marvin's church. But you still get the ocean swell of the Holy Spirit. And if you don't know how to swim, you'll drown.

What did I discover in the Holy Spirit swell?

That the human heart is on fire, and on fire with little pieces of heaven all over them. And when your heart has parts of heaven on it, that makes a sound. Have you heard it?

It doesn't sound like a muffled song that you're embarrassed to hear or sing. It sounds like a shouting from above. It comes in shouts, and praises, and people sounding off during the message, "Hallelujah!" and "Preach!" and "Yes, Lord!" It sounds like a unity of voices, sounding as one, with the power of angels and fire.

It is ear-piercing, gut-wrenching praise. A kick drum beating in your chest.

It looks like hands raised high in the air with no care of who is standing to the right or to the left.

It looks like dancing and spinning men and women, clapping their hands in an unexplainable joy. It looks like leaping, and I'm not using a figure of speech here. I mean literal leaping. It looks like wearing your best suit and tie, sweat pouring down, and you just don't care, because this is *church*. This is where you came to gather with the saints and participate in a hallelujah party.

All were invited.

It looks like a man running up and down the aisle. Why? Because he's worshipping. He's letting the music move him.

It looks like my cousin singing beside me, her hands raised, singing her heart.

Church blazes in my memory, like a scene from David's Psalms—I grew up living the Psalms. They are still so real to me because I lived those words of King David every Sunday morning. I think about Psalm 150, where it says:

Praise the LORD!
Praise God in his sanctuary;
praise him in his mighty heavens!
Praise him for his mighty deeds;
praise him according to his excellent greatness!

Praise him with trumpet sound;
praise him with lute and harp!
Praise him with tambourine and dance;
praise him with strings and pipe!
Praise him with sounding cymbals;
praise him with loud clashing cymbals!
Let everything that has breath praise the LORD!
Praise the LORD! (ESV)

Now take a moment and think about your church on Sunday morning. And I'm not trying to say my church is better than yours, I'm just saying that sometimes when you experience the Holy Spirit in church, your eyes see that church has nothing to do with the building or the technology or any of the fancy bells and whistles. The only thing that matters is the Holy Spirit.

Is the Spirit there?

And then, what is the Spirit about? When he moves, is he stagnant, or does he resemble the praise of the saints?

King David danced before the Lord. That's what we're told, and that's what I saw in the pews and from the pulpit: dancing before the Lord.

I heard messages that rained down upon our ears, heavy with passion and glory. King David talked about praising the Lord with clapping and raised hands. The Psalms tell us to sing a new song unto God. We're supposed to come before him with glad hearts making joyful sounds. When I was young, attending church, joyful sounds came from the Hammond B3 organ, and the textured chords of jazz, and lyrics that talked about the Good News of Jesus. These are the rousing sounds of the Holy Spirit—heaven sounds that bring tears of joy and laughter at the same time.

We discovered a new world at church. And it was dynamic. On the one hand it was this incredibly vivacious world, full of life and love and the grace of God. A world busting with creative freedom, with an invitation to discover the person God made me to be.

But on the other hand, it was a world with very clear rules. And those rules toughened us up. We didn't like them all. But it's like my brother Marvin says: we were taught the truth, and the truth stayed with us—it brought us up and made us men and women who hungered for God. And later in life, the truth set us free from legalism. Well, that last part was me.

Now, what I've just described is the passion side of church. And yes, it rings with a romantic kind of sound, doesn't it? Who wouldn't want to experience joy in music and dancing and singing? Who wouldn't want to stay all day long with family and friends, singing and dancing, eating and laughing, and experiencing a little bit of heaven on a Sunday afternoon? I may not attend a church that goes all day now, but I do miss the "event" of church in our culture. Most churches today reduce the event of the

BEBE WINANS

saints gathering and praising and receiving the Scriptures as if it were food from heaven itself, to something manageable, relevant to everybody's wants, something more in tune with everyone's busy schedules. When did we go off and get in such a hurry? There's no hurry in heaven.

LEARNING LOVE AT CHURCH

That's what church did for me and to me. It was an event that shaped my virtue, the way I saw the world; it shaped my voice, and it gave me a voice; it pressed its weight into me, and it gave me a platform on which to stand. It brought me up. It built me up. And it set me up.

Do I sound like I'm preaching?

Well, I'm sorry and I'm not. Preaching found its way into me. When I preach now, I'm preaching first to myself, something maybe we all need to do. Preaching to yourself gives you strength. It reminds and reassures you. It gives you a deep encouragement.

Can all this come from the event of church?

I believe so, yes. Because the event of church has nothing to do with a physical building. It has everything to do with *people*. People gathering to lift up the name of God—not themselves. And there's a beautiful power in leaving yourself at the door and focusing on someone else—someone like God, someone like your brother or sister—the ones you don't live with, the ones you live next door to.

The power of church dug deep into me and my siblings. We loved it. We may not have understood the spiritual power of church, but we did understand that church was a blast.

Can you imagine? Kids *loving* to go to church?

In today's world, parents have to force their kids to go to church and at the same time convince themselves to attend. But not in my day. It was exciting to go to church, to sing and dance and hear how much God loved us. We thought it was thrilling.

If Mom or Dad wanted to punish us really bad, all they had to say was, "You ain't going to church this week." That was awful, that was painful, but that's all they needed to say! We'd straighten up and fly right.

Church is where everything happened. Family, friends, the Lord, good food, all gathered in those halls, and my goodness, a joyful noise was heard and felt for miles away.

We loved church so much that for me and my brothers and sisters, our church family felt like our extended family. And I mean that in a very real sense—I'm not just being nostalgic. The adults at the church had full authority over us just like my birth parents. They could correct us verbally or with the belt. I think society calls this "corporal punishment," which makes me laugh. We simply called it a "whippin'," and to this day, to me and my generation, there is a big difference between discipline and abuse.

If it wasn't for that kind of loving from my parents and our church family, there's no telling where I and all the young people of my day would be. Our upbringing kept a high percentage of us out of jail, off drugs, in school, out of trouble, respectful to law enforcement, to teachers, and even taught us to care and respect our neighbors and strangers.

The love that I grew up hearing about in church was a love that corrected and disciplined when it needed to and taught us the good things of life, like family, faith, and friendship. I grew up hearing how love was patient and kind, slow to become angry, quick to forgive. It doesn't brag; it's not jealous. Love isn't selfish. It doesn't disrespect other people. It's not easily angered. It doesn't keep track of all the wrong things people do. It does not delight in evil; it delights in the truth. It always protects, and trusts, and hopes, and perseveres. Love never fails.

That is not a squishy kind of love. That's a love that requires us to listen to one another. It requires us to help one another. And when I say "one another," I'm not just saying your good friends, or the people you attend church with, or the people in your school or at your work. I mean e-v-e-r-y-o-n-e.

Love means the world to me. And I believe that's true for every human being, if we're really honest with ourselves. When I look back on the love I learned in church and from my family, I can see how so much of my life's story revolves around my understanding and application of love. My life and career can be traced by those times I learned hard lessons about love, when someone else loved me and taught me more about love, or when I was reminded about the brevity of life and the importance to walk in love, daily. What's so amazing about love is that it gives flight to other attributes, like compassion and forgiveness. And I know we miss that in today's world.

The old photographs of I.W. Winans and loved ones from our past that Marvin showed me stirred up images and smells and sweaty feelings of worship that felt like home. And as I think about it, the home I felt in that church began somewhere else.

The Mack church is a historical landmark in a beaten-down area of town on the east side of Detroit. But the founding of that church reaches even further back, before I was even a thought. It reaches into a time I hardly knew growing up in the Detroit of the twentieth century. Now I knew that it extended well beyond Detroit, into the Deep South of Centreville, Mississippi. Marvin and I can't be sure of his findings, but we're looking into it. But even the likelihood of it all is enough to give me pause for reflection.

WHERE HOME BEGINS

I'm the seventh son of David and Delores Winans, who once were David and Delores Glenn. Then Dad was convinced to change his name—to his rightful name, they say. And so he did, and all my siblings and I took on the name Winans and its history. The name touches two ethnicities and two histories and migrated to Detroit.

And I've read about the personal belongings many of those migrants took with them; simple things, really, whatever possessions they had, be it their King James Bibles, their steel guitars, or their congregations—they left for a new land and a new time, a new hope and a new future. And they risked their very lives for that freedom.

How incredible it is to think my family, who probably took on the name of their slave owners, left the Natchez Trace area and became the early human seeds of the Detroit that I now know and love. A friend told me the banjo was actually an instrument that originated in Africa, and that enslaved Africans were the first to use it in the New World.[9] Amazing how what is now known as a country music instrument actually influenced many genres, from bluegrass to boogie-woogie, to blues and rock and jazz and country. An African instrument, the forerunner and the shaper of much of the American music landscape. That instrument emigrated here and moved around, was played by many and used for all kinds of sounds. And just how that instrument was a seed for so much of the music many of us know and love today, so too were those families of the migration; they were the seeds of change, the seeds that formed and shaped early Detroit—banjo people strumming their songs, shaping the land with their lives.

That's what I was born into. That's the Detroit that shaped me. So in many respects, I was shaped by them— all the families, mine included, that set off for a new life. And their souls poured into Detroit as they brought along their Southern histories, their African and American legacies, and mixed it all together to form a dynamic land of music: Detroit.

A SENSE OF SONG AND HOPE

When I talked with my brother Marvin and asked him if he remembered the Detroit of our youth, he told me, "In Detroit, when Motown was in Motown, there was a sense of hope and an air of something special."

He reminded me that when we moved to the west side in 1966, it was not uncommon to see little Stevie Wonder performing on a street corner. It was nothing to go into a restaurant and see Gladys Knight or Marvin Gaye Sr., who later went on to pastor. Gaye's house wasn't far away from ours, and it was given to him by Berry Gordy, the founder of Motown Records. And like us, Marvin Jr. grew up in Pentecostal church singing in the choir. I wonder how strict his parents really were with him, because a holiness church meant rules and a whole different way of living.

We lived near Smokey Robinson's house, and we'd always try to get over there when it snowed hard because he paid well to have his sidewalk shoveled. We went to school with the sons of the Temptations. Music permeated the entire place. I lived music. There was a sense of song and home and hope that permeated the Detroit of my youth.

When Motown relocated to Los Angeles, its absence left a hole in Detroit. But this absence didn't affect Gospel music. Detroit is synonymous with Motown, with soul music and R&B, but let's not forget it's also a birthplace of Gospel music.

Some say Gospel music comes to us all the way from plantation holler songs, which reaches back to its roots, the African spiritual.[10] A holler song was usually sung by a lone worker out in the field; it was soulful, melancholy. There were also call-and-response work songs. I remember that scene from the Denzel Washington movie *Glory,* in which the black regiment gathered around the fire the night before a big battle and they sang old African spirituals—it was a moody scene of passion, despair, and hope.

They say if you Christianize an African spiritual, you get Gospel. I suppose that might be true. And it makes sense to me because Gospel music comes from the gut, it takes you over, and it points you to heaven—the only and best place for our hope in this world.

And maybe it was the Great Migration that brought all those sharecroppers—formerly enslaved—to this new place; maybe that was the infusion of so much passion and soul and music in Detroit. Maybe God filled the lungs of my great-grandfather, and his father, and gave them this town to preach in, to sing in. And here I find myself in this long line of preachers, hollerin' for heaven to come down and fill my soul—fill the souls of everyone.

I love Detroit because it's where I was raised. I love it because of its rich heritage in music, but I especially love Gospel music. That's all I knew as a young boy, and it's what I was steeped in as a teenager. It's what we sang in church, and it's what we sang around the house. And though some may suggest that Gospel music might come from the holler songs of the plantations, I can attest to how Gospel progressed through modern contemporary voices. Voices like the Clark Sisters, for example, who helped bring Gospel into the mainstream. They pioneered contemporary Gospel and won three Grammy Awards. Their song "You Brought the Sunshine" was a crossover hit and catapulted their careers. And Twinkie Clark? Well, she's known as the Queen of the Hammond B3 Organ. Whether you know it or not, you hear that instrument all over the musical landscape today.

Then there's the voice of Thomas Whitfield. Like the

Clark Sisters, he also helped shape contemporary Gospel music. He liked to mix different sounds together. He'd take jazz and classical music and fuse them together with Gospel sounds.

And I haven't even mentioned Andraé Crouch yet. He's Gospel music's most famous maestro. Perhaps you know him best for directing choirs for Michael Jackson and Madonna, but his influence goes so much deeper. He led the way for so many of us today in Gospel music by taking the traditional sounds and styles of Gospel music and mixing them with the newer secular music styles. You might say that the Gospel music family tree finds its roots in Andraé Crouch.

But I know Andraé from a more personal perspective. He discovered my brothers Ronald, Carvin, Marvin, and Michael when they were singing in church. He gave them their first major recording contract. When they received the contract from Andraé, Dad wanted to get the record done, but Andraé was dragging his feet. So, Dad took the initiative to drive my brothers to California. They stopped and performed in Tulsa, Oklahoma, on the way—to help pay for gas.

When they arrived, Andraé was out of town. But when he returned, he asked my brothers to perform for his father's church dedication. They sang "Are We Really Doing Your Will," followed by "The Question Is," which brought down the house. Andraé got them in the studio quick after that performance, and they recorded their first album, the self-titled *The Winans.*

MY FOUNDATION

This Detroit, this place that possessed a sense of hope, an air of song, that was my home and in a lot of ways my family. The root had grown deep. The foundation laid.

When I think back on my life as a young man growing up in Detroit, I think about foundations. If I wanted to be a singer but refused to learn the foundational rules and principles to music and singing, I wasn't going to get very far in the profession. In order to learn the foundational rules to music, I had to apply myself to them. I had to practice them—which Dad made us do. Sometimes, even on school nights, he made us practice until late in the evening.

I can remember Mom saying, "Skippy, they have to go to school in the morning."

And he'd say, "OK, well, let them get this last note right. Then they can go off to bed." Practice, practice, practice. It's part of building a foundation.

I can't make up what a whole note is and how many beats it gets. No, I spent time, just like my other siblings, studying other artists, such as Andraé Crouch, the Hawkins Family, the Caravans, the Mighty Clouds of Joy. Now, some of these artists you may not know. But let it be understood, my father allowed only Gospel music in our home. There may have been times as an older teenager I questioned this rule. But now, as an adult and parent, I understand Dad's rules completely. With the world we live in, with all the negative vibes swirling outside the doors, you need to ensure, as a parent, that there's as much positive inside the doors of your home.

So we listened to good music and musicians and singers who used positive lyrics in their songs. It was the positive, the good, the holy that Dad wanted influencing us.

In practicing, in listening to Gospel music, in listening—though at times grudgingly—to my parents, I was building a foundation.

As I tell my story through song, through a musical, through this book, over and over in my mind the word "foundations" rolls on like a song that my mother used to hum as she cleaned the house. My story is the story of having my house built upon the rock and not liking it sometimes. But despite my youthful ambition and struggles to always understand the value of what my parents were trying to build in us kids, the situations in my life revealed to me that what my parents set out to do was for my own good.

But foundations, I've found, are more than principles. They're made of real places and real people. Detroit, for example, was part of my foundation. It was more than just the city to me. And it was more than a place in which I grew up with my brothers and sisters. It was also a place where I learned the value of family, the value of hard work. It was a place where I learned the value of music.

Detroit was home to some of the best music our country has ever known. The Detroit music itself was a kind of foundation for us as a country. The music that came out of Detroit told the story of the love of God and of family, of ruin and of redemption. It was passionate and sweaty, glorious and raw.

DON'T LOSE YOUR WAY

It's hard to forget anything my dad told me. By now, you've got a good idea of the kind of man my dad was. And though he was a tough, firm man, he was also our biggest fan and advocate. We always knew Dad had our backs.

Earlier I mentioned how Dad encouraged me to know who I was before I walked through the door and into the outside world. If you know who you are, you won't lose your way. I've endured over five decades of life, and in many ways, I still feel as though I'm finding my way. But after so many years of hearing Dad in my ear, reminding me to be myself, to be the person God made me to be, in a lot of ways, being me now seems second nature.

That might sound a little strange, because aren't we all ourselves? And shouldn't that be the easiest thing to be?

Well, we live in a world in which every single person

now can be someone they are not. They can manipulate and curate their own digital existence and actually train themselves to be someone they are not. How easy is it, now, for you and me to lose our way simply because we've forgotten who we are? It sounds crazy. But crazy in today's world is too often true.

I've been thumbing through the history of the Winans family, taking pieces of the puzzle and snapping them together, seeing if all the pieces fit. In some ways, I'm surprised by the puzzle image that is taking shape. But in other ways, I'm not surprised at all. Because my God is the God of the unexpected. He uses all kinds of means and people to get things done in this world. And in my case, it looks as if he assembled a family out of the Deep South and the shackles of slavery to be a mouthpiece for a song. And that song is not a lonely hollerin' song from way out in the fields. It's a beautiful song of hope and acceptance and love. It's a song that reminds me that hope springs eternal because its source is heavenly. I'm happy to contribute a note or maybe a line to that song. And l hope if you hear it, you'll sing along and contribute too.

Even though Detroit played home to some of the most dynamic people and the most beautifully powerful music in the world, it wasn't going to launch my career, like I had dreamed it would when I was little. Whether or not I wanted to admit it to myself, I had been hoping to be a star since I even had a concept of what that was. And the stars I knew of and loved were stars in Detroit.

But God was going to have to take me elsewhere so I could learn what I needed to learn. I'd take my foundation with me, but I was headed away from the colorful and familiar Detroit toward something new and unexpected.

CHAPTER SEVEN

THE BUSINESS OF BROTHERS

And afterward,
I will pour out my Spirit on all people.
Your sons and daughters will prophesy,
your old men will dream dreams,
your young men will see visions.
Even on my servants, both men and women,
I will pour out my Spirit in those days.

—Joel 2:28–29

Being the baby boy is not very easy. Having six older brothers who think that they're really your dad and that they can tell you what to do, whenever they want? That gets old, quick. But I don't have to go down that road;

if you have older siblings, you know exactly where I'm coming from.

Even with all the not-so-fun stuff that accompanies being the baby boy, I still looked up to my older brothers. I remember like it was yesterday.

It was 1981, and our little house was buzzing with the commotion that comes with getting all dressed up to see your family members sing. But this time it wasn't church. My brothers Marvin, Ronald, Carvin, and Michael were giving a concert at Mercy College. And so, it was a kind of church, because they were giving a Gospel music concert. It was church, in a theater. Or so we thought.

My father always told us that before you can become an international star, you have to be a national star. And before you can become a national star, you have to be a regional star. And before you can become a regional star, you have to be a local star. There are levels of success that teach and prepare you for the next level.

My brothers had become local and regional stars. That night was their night.

So when it was time to leave, we heard the cattle call. Either Mom or Dad shouted every name of every individual who was living in the house.

"Come on down, it's time to go! We can't be late!"

My mother was the Queen of Worry. She always wanted to be on time.

Not only did we have to be on time, it was mandatory

that we looked good for the concert. That meant, for me, a tie—my Sunday best. My father used to tell us, "Boys, when you're representing God, you have to look that part. The best for the Best."

Those were the early days. Close to home. Singing to friends, family, church members, people in the community. And this was the family ritual. Put on your Sunday best and don't be late and support your family. Eventually, time and faithfulness will produce something great. That's what Dad and Mom impressed upon us.

In time, my brothers found success on the national level. They performed at the historical Fox Theatre, near downtown Detroit. This wasn't the church stage, which of course we all loved and adored. Nor was it the local college stage. This was the stage where Elvis Presley, Aretha Franklin, Smokey Robinson, Frank Sinatra, Sammy Davis Jr., Gladys Knight and the Pips, Liza Minnelli, and Stevie Wonder performed. This was the national stage.

And the theater itself? What can be said that hasn't been already? It was one of the five Fox theaters in the US in 1928. It had seen better days—it was a shell of itself in the eighties—and wasn't restored until a few years later. But still. My brothers were performing at the Fox Theatre. And we were all giddy with excitement.

Finally, we arrive at the concert. Right on time, maybe a little early (thank you, Momma!). And the place was electric. The old historic theater felt massive to me and full of wonder. And then the lights came up, and I saw the four of them standing on the stage, dressed crisply in matching suits. When they began to sing, it was like I had never heard them before. The Winans, my brothers, sang a smooth, more R&B-ish, more entertaining to the ears, more contemporary Gospel music than the traditional quartet Gospel sound popular at the time. The words were straight Gospel, but the music, the arrangement, the feel and sound—it sounded like smooth pop. I suppose that's why the crowd reacted the way they did.

Seeing my brothers on the stage stirred something inside me. I wanted to be up there. I wanted to hear the applause and the screams. I wanted to sing beneath the lights. I shouted, "This is incredible!" I was caught in the moment.

My brothers were up there onstage, and the whole audience was treating them like they were the Four Tops. This was weird to me because I was used to hearing the audience in the form of the congregation at our church go crazy with the Holy Spirit and sing and shout praises to God. But these people were screaming out for Jesus *and* my brothers. I remember one woman even threw her panties at them! We shouted out, "Oh, Jesus." Not as a praise but as an "Oh, help them, Jesus!" Lord of heaven, I prayed that my momma didn't see that. Momma didn't miss one thing; she surely didn't miss that.

We were so proud of my brothers. They had succeeded in

a way we never thought possible. It's funny now, because my father used to say that that style of music was the Devil's style of music. We used to laugh at Dad, because he always said that singers who sang Gospel music for a general audience "may be singing about Jesus, but they're one step away from the Devil."

Standing there in the moment left a mark on me—and that mark has never faded. My brothers sang one of their more popular songs, "The Question Is." One section of the lyrics goes:

Question is, will I ever leave you?
And the answer is, No, no, no, no...
Now the question is, will I do His will?
And the answer is, Yeah, yeah, yeah, yeah, yeah.

That song talks about deciding to follow Jesus, right then; deciding to serve Him, to stay faithful to Him. A great song. But sometimes lyrics catch you, and their meaning can bend in toward your own life situation, your own passions and thoughts. And for the briefest of moments, I felt the urgency of my desire to sing and to be known, just like my brothers. The moment might have been brief, but I remember that feeling vividly. It left a mark.

You can imagine, back at the house, after the concert, the celebration that ensued. We talked about how God had kept His promises. My father used to remind us about certain scriptures, about passages that enlightened us about success. One in particular says, "Whoever can be trusted with very little can also be trusted with much, and whoever is dishonest with very little will also be dishonest with much" (Luke 16:10). And my brothers were faithful—at church, at choir rehearsals, and at revival services. They sang the same way they sang at the Fox Theatre. They sang with the same passion in our church choir as they did in front of thousands of people. It was a blessed thing to talk about how God was faithful to His Word.

Now with my brothers' success with their album *Introducing the Winans*, touring was the next step. When that moment came, I was given the incredible opportunity to take over the choir at church. Not what I was looking for. But I was faithful. I carried on as my brothers traveled with my dad, who managed them during the early part of their career. At this point, they were national. And I was local.

Seeing my brothers find such success, I couldn't help but wonder, "When is it going to be my time?"

But as always, Momma was there to reassure me that God had a master plan. All He needed to bring His plan to fruition was patience—my patience. Oh, the virtue of patience. Such an ugly word when you're young. I was barely eighteen. And I was in a hurry for stardom.

Life isn't all glittery all the time, with dreams coming true. This truth we learned at a very early age, and we learned it at the hands and the example of our parents. Life is about hard work, whether that's working on your craft as a singer or musician, like everyone was in our family, or working a job at a grocery story. They taught us to do it with all our hearts, as worship to God. God has a plan, and so often it's hard to see, or it feels as though you might be just drifting.

But God wants us to move. He wants us to put our hands to the work in front of us, to be faithful in the small things first. And I needed to be faithful in small things, even when my brothers were up onstage living their dream. I'm thankful for those lessons now, but at the time that was a hard pill to swallow.

CROSSING OVER AT MUMFORD HIGH

Even with all the good lessons Dad was giving me, I didn't completely understand the choices that he and Mom made. I loved my family, and I knew that Mom and Dad had sacrificed for it; I still felt as though my parents had put their dreams aside for work. I kept dreaming that somehow my work and my passion could be the same thing. I wanted to sing more than I wanted to work, but some people managed to do both. I wanted to be one of those people, and I prayed that God would give me that opportunity.

And work did eventually come our way, but it wasn't the kind of work that I thought it would be. I was still learning. God saw to that. God, and our brothers Ronald and Marvin.

Ronald really believed that CeCe and I were special. He wanted to see CeCe and me use our talents, and he scouted out different opportunities for us. Even when we were in elementary school, Ronald made us form a group: CeCe, my brothers Daniel and Michael—before Michael was promoted and became one of the Winans—and I were the Winans Part Two.

One such opportunity Ronald found for us was the Mumford High School talent show. Mumford High was famous for their talent shows. Very talented students performed each year. Ronald's idea for our "group" was that we'd walk over from MacDowell Elementary School and perform at the Mumford High School talent show.

Boy, was I scared. But Ronald was convinced that we were prepared.

"What song should we sing?" I asked.

"'Tell Them,' by Andraé Crouch and the Disciples," replied Ronald.

But we couldn't just stand there and sing the songs; Ronald was having none of that. He had us moving like Gladys Knight and the Pips. CeCe was Gladys, and Michael, Daniel, and I were the Pips—the Christian version, that is!

What a proud moment that was for him and for us. The auditorium erupted in praise and applause for his invention.

Understand that singing a Gospel song at the talent show was courageous. But we did it, knowing that the audience was famous for throwing the acts they didn't enjoy off the stage. And those acts were singing secular, mainstream songs, not Gospel.

It was totally different than us singing in church. And that was OK. Though at the time it seemed like a major transgression. That was our first taste of "crossing over," I suppose. It felt good, and we had fun.

ANOTHER OPPORTUNITY

When the opportunity came for CeCe and me to travel to North Carolina and try out for The PTL Singers on Jim and Tammy Faye Bakker's *The PTL Club*, we were gung ho and ready.

PTL stood for "Praise the Lord," and Howard McCrary was the musical director for the television show. He'd gotten news of a few potential openings at PTL in Charlotte, North Carolina. Howard thought the opportunity would be great for CeCe and me to audition. None of us really understood the spotlight PTL would put us in. But I was ready to go for it.

My brothers told Howard that Dad would never let CeCe go all the way down to Charlotte. And they had every reason to be right. Dad didn't even let us boys go across the street and spend the night at our friends' houses—and we were boys! Daddy felt we were safe when we were in his house, because he could protect us. CeCe was the first—and spoiled—girl, the apple of Daddy's eye. So there was no way, we thought, that he would let her go all the way down south to audition for the show.

And what if she made the cut? Would she move down there? No way.

But Mom thought the opportunity was worth the experience. So Mom agreed to make the trip with CeCe and me. We took a Greyhound bus clear down to Charlotte. I'm old enough to know now that the Greyhound bus ride was not a 950-day journey. But it felt like it at the time. I don't care how old you are, a nineteen-hour bus ride can make you go half insane. All the stops. The people coming and going. The gas fill-ups. The awful food. I can paint a rosy picture now and say it was quite the adventure, but I'd be lying. It was a brutal bus ride, even though buses in the South had been desegregated for years by the time we made this trip in 1981.

But we didn't go insane. The excitement of the circumstances kept my mind churning the whole way down to Charlotte. The anticipation of what was to come was greater than the long journey to the faraway destination. When I stepped off that bus in Charlotte, I prayed for strength.

I do remember Momma saying, "I will never do this again."

I can say this now, as a father of two children, because I get it. What a sacrifice for me and CeCe. She left eight children behind for Daddy to care for, while she endured two starry-eyed teenagers on what felt like a one-thousand-day journey to Charlotte.

We all love our comfort zones. And my family and Detroit were my comfort zones. CeCe's too. Breaking away from your foundation, your rock of familiarity—that takes some doing. And it was no different for CeCe and me.

CHAPTER EIGHT

WHEN GOD DOESN'T MAKE IT HAPPEN

Hope deferred makes the heart sick,
but a longing fulfilled is a tree of life.

—Proverbs 13:12

I can still remember the audition today. Not the nitty-gritty, just the roller coaster of feelings. And the smell and heat of the South in April. In Detroit in April, the sun is still sleeping, and the ground is still covered in snow.

For the audition, CeCe sang an original and upbeat song that my brother Marvin wrote called "The Giver of Life." I thought that was the wrong song for her to choose. But she sang it anyway.

I thought this whole thing out. White Christians?

Hmm. The "right" song would be a traditional hymn. I had the perfect song: "He Looked Beyond All My Faults (Amazing Grace)" by Dottie Rambo.

Dottie Rambo was a white singer/songwriter from Kentucky; she'd been around a long time and written thousands of songs. They weren't chump songs either. They were hugely popular Christian songs in the white American church, such as "We Shall Behold Him" and "I Go to the Rock." I thought this Pineville crowd would certainly know her stuff. I thought it was a good plan to sing a familiar, well-loved song.

It was a nerve-racking experience. After our auditions, I wanted to find out right away whether I'd—we'd—made it. But things didn't unfold in that way.

THE BLUR OF DREAMS

I'd love to opine on the particulars of that audition. But I can remember only bits and pieces. Maybe it all washed away on the bus ride back home. Here's what I do remember.

The audition was not well attended. Jim and Tammy weren't there. And there wasn't a large crowd of onlookers. The audition space was a simple boxy kind of a room with a keyboard and keyboard player.

"Are you ready?" they asked.

You answered. You sang your song.

"Thank you. There's the door."

Poof, you were done. In and out.

No one applauded you when you finished. No three judges with star-studded pasts in the music business stood in front of you waiting to critique you or run you out of the room. Just your sister and your momma waiting to take you home on a dingy Greyhound bus the next morning.

I also vaguely remember the other hopefuls—people like me, hoping for a break. About twenty people from across the country descended upon Pineville to make their voices heard. Twenty people, for six available slots. CeCe and I were the only chocolate drops.

Howard thought we did well. I think he might have used the term "wonderfully." Or maybe that's what I wanted to believe he said. Either way, very soon we'd find out if he was correct.

I remember walking around the PTL campus and pinching myself at the thought that I was—we were—inside one of the biggest television networks (at that time). We ate a catered meal right on site! We stayed overnight at some cheap hotel, although back then it felt like high-class, because a Holiday Inn was the Ritz to me.

When I close my eyes and try to remember the trip, it's like looking through the window of the Greyhound bus: a blur of trees, sky, and open fields, with some singing thrown in.

The next morning, we hopped back on the Greyhound, and it ran us back the many miles to Detroit. On the ride back home, I prayed hard: "This is it, God. This is it. Make it happen, Lord." In my mind, the trip made me feel as though I'd arrived in Hollywood. I had finally reached a place that possessed the potential for my gift to be heard by multitudes. The audition was my gateway to stardom—that's what I kept telling myself.

When we returned home, our whole family was curious about the trip and the audition. We told the story, which I'm sure was more dramatic and colorful than the one I just described to you. Everyone seemed genuinely hopeful for us. I was eager to hear the great news that we'd both made the show.

In my mind unfolded all the dreams a young eighteen-year-old has about stardom and fame. The excitement of moving out of the state, of traveling and doing music, just like my brothers were doing. That was the dream.

Then, on a normal kind of day, the call came.

There was good news and bad news.

They loved CeCe, but they didn't like me that much.

They wanted CeCe, and they passed on me.

That day was the first time I felt that God didn't have ears.

The news introduced a new scenario, one I'm not sure even Mom and Dad had discussed. CeCe was going to travel back down to Pineville, North Carolina, and live there and perform on *The PTL Club* by her soon-to-be sixteen-year-old self?

"I'm not going to let my baby girl go down there by herself," Daddy said.

What happened next surprised me, even as the words leapt from my mouth. "Daddy," I said, "just let her have this opportunity, and I'll go down with her, and I'll find a job. I'll work in a grocery store or something."

I can't really explain why I was thinking that. But that's the truth of it. And for some strange reason, Daddy agreed. But even though Mom and Dad decided, to everyone's surprise—especially mine and CeCe's—that this move was going to happen, it wasn't without reservations.

My brothers were livid. Marvin and Ronald were angry that my father said yes. When I talk to Marvin about it today, he remembers being excited for us and wanting us to succeed. So perhaps what I remember as anger really is just their disbelief that Dad allowed us to go. Dad didn't allow them to do much of anything on their own. And they were the older boys. So the question for them was, "How can you be so strict with us, and then allow our fifteen-year-old sister to move to another state?"

Dad quickly reminded them that he was the father, and he made the final decision.

We all had to settle in and realize that this was a miracle—God was definitely working His plan. It might not sound like an act of God to you, but in my household, this was on par with God speaking to Moses from the burning bush. I'm not sure that made our house a holy ground, but it kind of felt like it.

Even though I spoke up and suggested they let CeCe go, I still felt as though I'd gotten the short end of the stick. Maybe I'd gone crazy on that bus ride.

Mom and Dad picked up on my dejection, and their strength and encouragement helped me endure. I knew in that painful moment, because of their example throughout my life, that I was going to be OK. What a blessing it was to have two parents in the house. Even though my mom and dad had their issues, they were there for us, and for each other. Both parents play a role. And when one is absent, there's a void you can't fill; I get that. And that void contributes to the difficulty in growing into your total potential. When things are incomplete around you, it's hard to be whole. I was fortunate that my parents gave me the opportunity to be a whole person.

They said, "BeBe, you *can* sing. It's going to be OK."

They've always been my number one advocates, Mom especially. My siblings knew she had a soft spot for me. And I'll take that soft spot over most anything this world has to offer. I was grateful then, as I am now, at how loving Mom and Dad were to me and have always been in tough situations. They encouraged us all, and loved us all, and they did it with firm words, and tough love, and God's Word ready on their lips.

Even though they encouraged me, it was still tough to watch one of my closest siblings get excited and prepare to do the very thing I'd set my heart on.

Dad said to me, "Benjamin, you have everything inside of you that you need to make it in this world. Don't sit here and wait for something to happen. Go, work, sing. See what God does with your willingness to serve and work hard."

It was here that the words to the lyrics that I'd write decades later began to take shape:

Born for this
Destined for greatness
Am I prepared for this
You're strength for my weakness
I know life's not always easy
Question if it's worth the risk
But deep inside something whispers
Yes, you were born for this

But at the time, I could only wonder, "Born for what? Born to watch other people achieve their dreams?"

The tough news, and the even tougher living scenario that I myself had suggested, taught me a hard but good lesson. When man says no, that's never the final word. My faith taught me that if God is for me, who can be against me? A negative situation can be a pause or something God uses to get you going, to inspire you to keep going. In that career moment for me, Jim and Tammy put a pause on my singing career, but they didn't end it.

With my life lesson in tow, I still had to face reality.

I remember us packing, getting a moving truck, and filling it up with stuff, even though we didn't own much since we were still living in our parents' house.

This was God's will for me. He'd just parted the Red Sea. I was on my way to the promised land, and it just happened to be Pineville, North Carolina.

CHAPTER NINE

RAISING MY VOICE AND SEIZING OPPORTUNITY, WHATEVER THE CIRCUMSTANCE

Rejoice in the Lord always. I will say it again: Rejoice!

—Philippians 4:4

Everyone at PTL was eager to promote CeCe from the beginning. They loved showing off her talent.

"You'll not be disappointed," Tammy said to the live and television audiences.

What she didn't have to point out was the fact that CeCe was African American. I suppose they wanted to share with their audience that they were becoming diverse and that the audience could look forward to more of this on the horizon.

Even though Tammy was trying to show that PTL was

diverse, singling out CeCe was a little jarring. It felt as though the Bakkers were just getting used to the idea of having black people on their show. Tammy had every good intention, and genuinely loved people, and most certainly loved CeCe. But when you come from a place where race isn't pointed out to a place where the color of your skin makes you feel as though you come from another planet, it takes some getting used to.

After making sure everyone knew CeCe was African American, Tammy segued into the hymn "Blessed Assurance." Some of the lyrics of that song read: "This is my story, this is my song / Praising my Savior, all the day long." Well, that was only true of one of us. I was bagging groceries and stocking shelves all the day long. CeCe was the one singing praises all day long.

Howard caught up with me early on and asked how things were going. I was struggling.

"Did I make this trip and agree to help CeCe and live here, all so I could work at the grocery store?" I lamented.

Howard tried to lay Mom and Dad's advice on me. But I already knew it.

"Yes, I know God has a plan for my life. But when am I going to see that plan unfold? And is it going to unfold here? Have I made a mistake?"

It was good to have Howard around, someone who knew us and a safe person I could open up to about my struggles.

Questions, questions, questions plagued me.

But Howard encouraged me and informed me of an opportunity in the choir. He led the choir, so he knew that this could potentially be a stepping-stone to something more. But when you're eighteen years old, you don't always see that far ahead. Most of the time teens are too busy fretting about today to find the joy on the horizon of tomorrow. And that was true of me. I didn't know what seemed worse: the grocery store or the choir. But I reminded myself of the opportunity. Maybe this was part of God's plan for my life.

Not being hired for what I thought I was born to do wasn't easy. Rejection is normal in life, but I've come to understand the best part of life is surviving rejection and letting it become the fuel that takes you straight to your destiny.

WHISPERING MY SONG

It wasn't long after my lament to Howard about my situation as a bag boy that he invited me to practice with the choir along with the PTL Singers on a Sunday morning at the Barn, which was a beautiful facility that was sometimes used for special evening performances. And these performances were televised. On this particular Sunday morning, CeCe was going to lead a verse of the old Fanny Crosby hymn "Blessed Assurance." Howard had planned for me to step out on CeCe's verse near the end and riff on it. Now, if you don't know this hymn, you really should find an old hymnal and read the words. They're lovely. The second half of the second verse reads:

Angels, descending, bring from above
Echoes of mercy, whispers of love.

When that moment came in the song, I gave "whispers of love" all the love I had inside me. It was one of those moments that freezes in your mind, and you revisit it often—especially when your life and career get you down, you remember those moments when you stood shining before God, feeling His joy, feeling His gift work in your bones, feeling the satisfaction that comes from exercising that gift, and then you feel all right again. That's the kind of moment I'm talking about. It was a moment that changed my life and my understanding of how our timing is really sometimes not the right timing at all.

As God would have it, Jim walked from the set and over to the choir. Then he asked, "Who did that? Who sang those whispers of love?" I sheepishly admitted to the riff, thinking I'd crossed the line. There I was, wasting my only chance to use my gift, even though it was with the choir—something I wasn't thrilled about—and I botched it. Now I was in hot water for trying to add a little soul to the song.

But I was wrong. Jim was not angry. He loved it. He thought it was full of the Holy Spirit. He said he wanted more of whatever I was doing on the song. And then he turned to me and told me that I was now one of the PTL Singers.

I didn't know how to respond.

CeCe ran over to me and hugged me.

I stammered over my words, trying to thank Mr. Bakker. All I could do was thank him over and over again.

SINGING DUETS AND WORLDLY SH**

CeCe and I never dreamed we would sing duets together. It was early on in our time with Jim and Tammy Bakker that the opportunity presented itself. Even though the whole Charlotte experience initially made my heart bounce back and forth between feeling rejected and embracing the hope of possibility, I tried to keep my faith. When circumstances shifted, it was faith that gave me the strength to walk into the possibilities—new, scary, very white. God thrust me into it. I seized it.

Our first appearance on the show was a duet, and it was a doozy.

We were standing side by side, all tense and fidgety, getting ready to sing together on live television for the first time. The producer shouted for people to take their places and for the lights to come up.

"It's happening. It's really happening!" I wanted to pinch myself, but I was so focused on the moment.

Then, from the back of the set, Tammy walked in and stood right next to me. I was not ready for that. I stood as straight as an arrow. Nervous. Trying to keep it together. She could sense my nervousness, I think. She said, "Everything's going to be just fine. God will be our confidence."

And then Jim entered. "Good morning," he said to everyone right as the countdown started.

"Ten, nine, eight..."

Jim kept talking, reassuring us that God was going to use us and that we'd be a blessing to the masses.

"Seven, six, five..."

The producer continued the countdown and Tammy, who was standing between me and the piano, placed her finger on the piano. Then the lid of the piano slammed down on her hand.

"Shit!" Tammy said it so loud, I couldn't believe it. CeCe and I were like deer in headlights, full of disbelief, looking straight ahead. But the countdown continued. This was live television, in mere seconds.

But in that split second, my whole world shifted like an earthquake had moved it off its mark.

The producer ended the countdown, and the lights came up. And without missing a beat, Tammy greeted the viewing audience, "Praise the Lord!"

"Shit!" and "Praise the Lord!" within the span of a few seconds. What had just happened? Were my ears playing tricks on me?

The show went on, and CeCe and I and the rest of the singers sang the opening song. Afterward, I wondered if anyone other than CeCe and I had heard Tammy curse. I wondered what we'd gotten ourselves into. I even questioned whether we had made the right choice in joining the singers. You'd think my first thought would have been about how we sounded and if people seemed to like it. I immediately asked CeCe, "Do you think anybody else heard Tammy curse on air?" CeCe didn't think so and also shared my surprise and questioned what we'd gotten ourselves into.

"Shit!" and "Praise the Lord!" in the same sentence from a Christian woman?

Was I living in a nightmare? But this wasn't a dream at all! This was my new reality. We were a long way from home and the church and Christianity I thought I knew. My world was upside down. Everything about our PTL experience was different. These people spoke differently, and they drank different drinks that were not of the Lord! But I'll get into the drinking later.

GROWING UP IN GRACE

The swearing-Tammy incident was an event for me. It rocked my world. But it pushed me into discovering some of these truths on my own. I saw that there was more grace in some of these gray areas than I once believed. Church life and grace life grow and morph with you. When you're a kid and church is your everything, you accept it and love it and continue on with your life.

But when you embark upon adulthood, you begin to see things from the new vantage point of age and experience. Sure, I loved church when I was younger. I still love church. It's a central part to the rhythm of my life. But at the same time, as much as I loved the experience of church when I was younger, the rules that accompanied church felt heavy at times.

CeCe couldn't wear makeup as a teenager. That was worldly. And young men did not wear beards. We dressed our best, because Jesus cared what we looked like when we sang our songs to Him. And music? Gospel music was it. Secular music? No way. That was worldly music. You risked going to hell if you listened to secular music. That was the Devil's tool for evil.

My dad didn't allow us to say certain things; certainly we were not allowed to use profanity. We even couldn't say things like, "Shut up"; yes, that was pushing it. Living in the world, you're going to hear everything. But that was the world, Dad said. We didn't speak like the world. But when we moved to Charlotte, I realized that these brothers and sisters used curse words. Were they going to hell? Were they really even Christians at all?

How you grow up shapes your worldview. And when you step out of the world you know into a new place, with new people, your eyes open. Sometimes that's good, sometimes bad, but always a revelation. When CeCe and I stepped off the bus with Mom, stepping foot in Charlotte for the first time, our eyes were opened. In many ways it was our first steps into liberation.

Slowly, CeCe and I were liberated from all those silly rules that kept blinders on us. PTL was makeup land. The world of cosmetics. CeCe became a cosmetic girl. No more using Vaseline as lip gloss. Now it was real makeup—the kind in the commercials! Worldly! Oh, Lord!

On one occasion, our entire group of singers went out to eat at Bennigan's after doing a show. We sat in the tavern section. I looked around and thought, "Oh, Lord, what am I getting myself into?" CeCe and I didn't drink alcohol. That was Devil water. We all took our seats, and the man next to me began taking drink orders. When he came to me, I told the group, "Hey, y'all, I'm a Christian. I'll have a Diet Coke." Everyone laughed.

I could not believe my eyes. Real Christians sat on each side of me, drinking alcoholic beverages. I was drinking Diet Coke, but I still feared going to hell for sitting in that sinful place with these people who called themselves Christians and drank ALCOHOL!

I still don't drink alcohol. I prefer an icy ginger ale. But I don't judge Christians with integrity sitting around, having a great time, and enjoying a beer or glass of wine. Some will say I have matured as a Christian, and others will say I am a backslider.

The Lord has brought me a long way, and my eyes were opened with regard to how to get along with saints who were raised differently and also love the Lord. In that moment when Tammy screamed, "Shit!" growth happened. It was confusing, but it was also the beginning of a liberation. I realized that God's family doesn't look or act like any one kind of person. You can be a white Southern lady or man in a Bennigan's enjoying a beer or glass of wine and still be part of God's family. You can be a black man in the South, sipping some ginger ale and still be part of God's family. I learned that God's family was much bigger than Detroit. All these years later I can say emphatically that God's family is bigger than any one person's experience or context. God only cares that you love Him and that you love others.

I enjoyed watching my mom and dad step into the same liberation over the years. Once my mother was at home singing while she dusted the furniture. My brother Ronald walked through the room but stopped when he heard what Momma was singing.

"Momma, is that Whitney Houston you're singing?"

"Oh, is it?" she replied, playing dumb.

"Yeah, Momma. You're singing 'Where Do Broken Hearts Go' by Whitney Houston." She kept on humming.

So there you have it. Even my own mother can enjoy Whitney's music. And who couldn't, right?

Music was something else that expanded when we arrived in Charlotte. Being part of *The PTL Club,* CeCe and I met many singers, including Sandi Patty and Amy Grant, both early pioneers in the Contemporary Christian Music (CCM) scene. Amy Grant went on to be one of the first highly successful CCM singers to cross over into the general (or "secular") market.

For young singers with high hopes and dreams for our own careers, meeting real-life singers was so impactful. It showed me that the church—the family of God—didn't look only like Detroit. It looked like Charlotte, and New York, and Nashville. Everyone I met loved Jesus, but they were so different from me and CeCe. I was young, but not too young to realize that this experience was going to be a stepping-stone that would change my life, and my understanding of people, forever.

Our performance of the song couldn't have gone better. The reaction of the crowd was overwhelming. In spite of all the pressure, we stayed true to who we were.

After the show ended and the lights came down, Jim and Tammy ran to us and hugged us over and over, telling us how wonderful we'd done. Jim kept saying how he knew we'd do well. He was like a mini-prophet. He told us God was going to do great things with us. But all I could think about was Tammy's language and how relieved I was to have that number over and done with.

It was a confusing time for me, as a growing young man and as a singer. I wanted to excel, to take advantage of the opportunity, but I was conflicted because Christians in the South were so different than in Detroit. But the longer we performed with the folks on PTL, the more comfortable it all became. Although I didn't start cursing, I did begin to flourish where God planted me.

CHAPTER TEN

I LIKE YOUR VOICE,
NOT YOUR COLOR

For the Spirit God gave us does not make us timid,
but gives us power, love and self-discipline.
—2 Timothy 1:7

Our performance caused quite a stir. The next day at the offices the phones rang off the hook. And it wasn't people calling in to say how well CeCe and I had performed. There were some of those calls—probably a good mix of bad and good. But some of the bad were really bad—accompanied by cursing and harsh language about us blacks being on the show. We even received threats.

Tammy reacted to the negative much differently than Jim did. Jim understood and appreciated that they were doing something different with the show, something no other evangelical, fundamentalist Christian program was doing. He half expected there to be some pushback. He always said that when you do things that make people feel uncomfortable, they are going to squirm. And he was quick to point out that Jesus often made people, especially religious leaders, feel uncomfortable. But I'm not sure he expected people from a supposedly Christian audience to call and make threats. When he was told about the negative calls and the threats, he tried to keep it quiet, away from Tammy and us, but Tammy found out. She always found out.

I'm quite sure a few "those sons of a bitches" spilled from Tammy's mouth when she found out about the threats and negative calls. She was our white mother. She was going to have none of this from "ignorant rednecks" who "don't know good music when they hear it." We were her children, and she was going to protect, come hell or high water.

I loved Tammy for being Tammy. She took some getting used to, but her heart was pure gold. And she didn't take nothing from nobody. She was always herself, loud and proud. My mom taught me life and God and virtues and music. Tammy taught me to be myself, always. And not to worry about what someone else says or does. It was a lesson in confidence—not that I needed any when it came to singing. In fact, my dad might have argued that I needed a little bit of humility. And he was probably right.

But confidence in your giftedness doesn't always translate to confidence in who you are when the lights go out. And that's what I picked up from Jim and especially from Tammy. They believed in me and in CeCe when it wasn't cool or advantageous. But their pioneering spirit taught me to go with my gut and believe in myself and the ideas and dreams that I have and to push on through.

When you discover that people don't like you because you're black, that's something different. And we did find out about the negative calls and threats. And it wasn't because we couldn't sing. We were two black sore thumbs sticking out in a white world of pine trees and cowboy hats.

When I called Mom in Detroit to complain about how hard it was sometimes to still be called "Negroes," "niggras," or "colored," Mom took the negative and turned it into a positive. She told us that we were given the opportunity to shine a light in the South and to pray for them. CeCe was her amen corner and did just that.

STEPPING OUT ON THE BRANCH

Once things got rolling on the show, I started to spread my wings a little, relax and hang out with some of the guys. My friends saw it too and began encouraging me to have a beer and chill out. They'd offer me beer, and I'd try to be polite and decline. They knew I didn't drink.

I half believed they did it just to get a rise out of me. I told them that where I came from, when you're saved, you drink Kool-Aid or iced tea or Coke or Vernors, which is a ginger ale—my personal favorite. But I did do other things with them. I started doing things that no black man in his right mind would do: white-water rafting.

When my mom got wind of my white-water rafting, she told CeCe to remind me that I was black. Where I came from, sports were basketball or football or bowling. But the guys I hung out with egged me on, telling me I needed to be more adventurous. I'd tell them that what you guys call "sport" or "adventure," we call "dangerous." But even though I put up a verbal fight, I still went white-water rafting with them. There is truth to the adage "Bloom where you're planted." I could spend time rolling my eyes over Charlotte and wringing my hands about the South, or I could step out of my comfort zone and get to know the folks I worked with.

I wonder what our culture would be like if we spent more time listening to one another, more time hanging out and eating with one another, more time trying what others like. I wonder if there'd be less hate and more understanding. I wonder if there'd be more fun and less fighting. The part of me that went white-water rafting remained with me. And for that I'm thankful. We're all born to fly. We're born naturally curious. We're wired for friendships, for deep relationships. But those relationships will never come unless we're willing to step off the branch and fall a little bit.

SEXY FOR THE LORD

Our horizons were broadening everywhere I looked. Some horizons I was eager to have broadened. Others took me by surprise.

Old garments from our upbringing changed, not only with the times but with the Bakkers. Tammy had a more "sexy" approach for Christian women's apparel. She commented one day on how good the singers looked and added a suggestion to the person in charge of wardrobe: raise the hemline a little for the ladies because there was nothing wrong with showing a little bit of leg on television. She made sure it happened. CeCe and I welcomed the change to being "fashion forward for the Lord." We knew the day we wore the new styled attire on television our mom would see and the phone would ring and she would remind us that we were "Holy and Sanctified" and that we were responsible to show that with our clothes. The Bakkers did allow us to voice our opinion, and soon we found a balance with wardrobe. I came to enjoy Tammy and Jim; they were willing to listen to what we had to say. We found common ground that made our relationship special.

But Tammy wasn't finished.

When I see today all the beautiful pictures of CeCe on albums and on television shows, her makeup is flawless, and that's thanks to PTL. Before PTL entered our lives, CeCe didn't wear makeup because in our church upbringing, it was a sin. Yes, wearing makeup was a *sin*.

Tammy was famous for her makeup—maybe more famous for too much makeup. "Makeup," she said, "is a good girlfriend." Again, our white momma was telling us to do things that our Detroit momma would never have allowed. We were scared and confused but also a little excited—at least I was. Not that I wanted God and the ladies looking at my chest, but I suppose those Southern friends of mine, with their outdoorsy adventures, rubbed off on me.

Some chapters of our lives we never want to read again. Some we reread the first chance we get. I like this chapter of my life. It was hard in some respects: threats because of the color of my skin, feeling unsafe and unsure, singing for the first times on national television.

On the other hand, when you have faith, you can soar above all that. But how did we soar? The answer sounds simple, but living it out was anything but. I let God carry me. The writer in Isaiah says:

Even youths shall faint and be weary,
and young men shall fall exhausted;
but they who wait for the LORD shall renew their
    strength;
they shall mount up with wings like eagles;
they shall run and not be weary;
they shall walk and not faint. (Isaiah 40:30–31, ESV)

I said prayers of hope. I cried out to the God of hope, the One God who sustains the whole universe with His words. There's something about uttering a prayer that fills a person with something special. The Bible says there's also power in the name of Jesus. When we cry out, "Jesus, help me," we're crying into heaven and that power, that glory, touches us and lifts us.

Even in my overzealous ambition, I prayed for strength to fit in to this new place. And God delivered me hope and encouragement, and He gave me the confidence I needed—not only to sing in front of people but to actually be with people off the stage, people who were different than me. People who grew up different than me. People who couldn't sing a lick of Stevie Wonder—Lord have mercy. Hope is a great word. But it opens up its treasure only when you step off the branch and let yourself fall so that you can fly.

CHAPTER ELEVEN

THE ONLY THING YOU KNOW IS THE NEEDLE

Jesus said, "Father, forgive them, for they do not know what they are doing."

—Luke 23:34

I might have been spreading my wings with my newfound freedom, but that new freedom came with a lot of new world-shattering realities.

Though I understood that CeCe and I were two of the few black people on a white Christian praise and worship program, it still took some getting used to. In Detroit, no one called me a Negro or colored. But in Charlotte, this was more common than I ever thought possible. And this was in the eighties! I thought we were past all that. But apparently my mom was right. The South was just slow—in more ways than one.

And though I like the idea of celebrating how different we are, and even laughing at some of the idiosyncrasies of white and black people, there are certainly negative and hurtful stereotypes, like every black man is a drug dealer or every black woman might work the corner.

A DETOUR

Four black people were part of PTL at the time, including a wonderful, funny elderly black woman who attended the Sunday church services at the Barn on the grounds of PTL. She was always a burst of energy and encouragement to all, but especially to me and CeCe. I remember one Sunday as I approached her to chat for a moment, I noticed she wasn't her perky self.

"Hello," I said as I walked up to her. "Is everything OK? What's wrong?"

Her reply will always bring confusion and laughter to my soul.

"Well," she said, "on my way to church, as I was singing and praising the Lord for all His mighty works, out of the clear blue sky a car struck mine! Thankfully, although I was shaken up, I wasn't physically harmed.

"Now, like all drivers do when this happens, I began to gather my insurance information and proceeded to get out of the car and handle the matter. But before I could do any of that, the car pulled off into the unknown."

"A hit-and-run?" I asked in shock.

"Yes, Brother BeBe, it was a hit-and-run."

I felt awful for her. I don't know if there was a confused look on my face to cause her to encourage me not to worry, but what came out of her mouth next set me up for life!

"Don't worry, brother," she said. "When they pulled away, I started praying and asked God to cause whoever the individual was, that when he or she arrived at work Monday morning, they'd begin to speak in tongues!"

If you didn't grow up in the kind of church I did, one that believed in all the gifts God had given to His church, speaking in unknown tongues is one of those gifts.

Think about it. A woman or man walks into their job Monday morning, says hello to everyone, and in the next breath causes everyone to stare, because that sentence she or he just blurted out, no one in the building can understand!

I'm glad some prayers God understands but does not answer for our benefit.

WE'RE DIFFERENT, AND LET'S LEAVE IT AT THAT

What I learned through my PTL experience, and the experience of others, is that we should pray for understanding and be willing to allow time to bring us the answers we want. Waiting for understanding can invite hurt. That process of waiting for understanding can turn into a waiting game of pain. But the alternative to waiting for understanding is lashing out in ignorance. And our world has enough of that already.

Jim and Tammy did things that I didn't understand or agree with, but through *patience* and *love* I accepted and leaned on God's understanding. Jim and Tammy said some things that made you say, "Umm...what?" But I can testify that the love of God was a big part of their hearts. Changing the way people viewed race was a mission for them at a crucial time on the PTL Network.

Jim and Tammy realized that change started with them. I believed Jim was going to be a catalyst for people to alter the way his audience thought about black people in general, not just on their show.

But part of me wrestled with confusion. One minute it felt as though Jim and Tammy wanted the world for us. And they did. But the next minute, it felt manipulative. It felt as though we were being used to set the show apart, to draw an audience.

CHAPTER TWELVE

THE SCARY STEPS OF DOING
WHAT YOU LOVE

"You are the light of the world. A town built on
a hill cannot be hidden."

—Matthew 5:14

I don't look over my shoulder enough and realize how far
I've come, how God's provided for me in every situation. I
sometimes lose sight of His blessings.

It's easy to keep looking down the road at what we hope
will come and miss the beauty and joy of this moment
right now.

I was definitely in the moment now at PTL. Singing
with CeCe for the first time on *The PTL Show* as a featured
duo was something that never crossed my mind. It just

materialized. The exhilaration told me I was in the right place, but so much was unknown.

Our situation escalated when Jim had the insane idea that we sing a popular song from a movie. It was risky, but it was the single decision that launched CeCe and me into a place we had only dreamed about.

When I think back on that opportunity, I'm thankful for my faith and the strength it gave me to raise my voice.

Sometimes we can say such a thing and it can ring hollow, or we just say it to fill in a conversation. But when I say my faith gave me strength, I mean that in a very real sense. My faith was something instilled in me by my family.

And whenever I needed encouragement or a kick in the rear, my family was always there to give it to me. And not just my parents. My crazy siblings also supported me. We supported one another. That's what faith looks like.

A strong faith isn't just this thing out there floating around in the air. It's tangible. It manifests itself in real people and real help given by those real people, and real words of support and real actions of comfort. In the New Testament book of James, the writer says, "In the same way, faith by itself, if it is not accompanied by action, is dead" (James 2:17).

Faith is believing, and then acting like what you believe is so.

When you actually break down the words of a cliché like

"my faith strengthens me," you realize that it means that people who believe like you, who love you, people who want to see the best for you, actually did something real to help and push you. You realize that when you see faith pour out of those people whom you love, you are seeing the seeds of humility poured out.

Because how beautiful is it to see others love you in such a way?

How beautiful to realize that the strength you receive in order to reach a goal or dream comes from other people. A special indebtedness remains. Not an indebtedness that feels heavy, but something that is light and motivates you to make everyone proud.

When Jim got this crazy idea for CeCe and me to perform this song, we knew it was risky. But at the same time, it felt like the push I needed to get out there in a place and situation I had no control over and let God show me what He had in store.

After we finally got our footing on the show, our time and involvement there felt good, given how odd things felt when we first arrived.

NOT WHAT I EXPECTED

We were getting paid for our performances, and all was good. I was, in many respects, living the dream. I was doing what Mom and Dad and Marvin and Ronald said

I should do. They had told me to wait, and it had been so hard. But so worth it. Jim came to the PTL Singers rehearsal and asked Howard, the musical director, if he knew the song from *An Officer and a Gentleman.*

"What is that?" I wondered. "Oh no, that's not a movie, is it? Those things are evil. They are *secular.*"

The song to which Jim was referring was "Up Where We Belong," which was sung by the rock and blues singer Joe Cocker. The lyrics, well, let's just say they lend themselves to being bent toward Christian themes, as he sings about love lifting us up so we can be "far from the world below."

Although Jim wanted us to sing a Christianized version of the song, this was our ticket to hell. That was the call we were going to get from Mom and Dad when they watched us sing it on the show. That call never came, but the thought of receiving such a call was in my mind.

Our upbringing, as solid as it was, was rooted in legalistic Christianity. Remember, when my dad stopped singing for his quartet, he did so because when you started attending a holiness church, it was understood that your life reflected it. You didn't gamble, or smoke, or drink, or run around clubs, or sleep around, or listen to worldly music. No—you were a church man or woman now. And it had to show. Those same rules, manifested in different ways, hung around when we grew up. The tension of being asked to sing this worldly song was countered by a voice in the back of my head, which sounded a lot like Dad. It was enough to drive a person insane. It was hard to let go of some of those rules, walk outside our old boundary lines, and do something I knew might be looked at with judgment from family and friends back home.

So, even though CeCe and I didn't know the song, we agreed to sing it live on the show. They changed some of the lyrics to make them more Christian.

I thought we'd sing it and that would be it. But after we sang it, everyone went crazy. The response was immense and totally unexpected. Singing that song was our turning point.

Shortly thereafter, Jim Bakker started his own record label for PTL. The natural next step was for CeCe and me to record. My brother Daniel Winans, my sister-in-law Vickie Winans, and a good friend, Marvie Wright, came to Charlotte to sing on our record. Bill Maxwell, who had produced Andraé Crouch, produced the record.

I'd been around Bill when he worked with Marvin and my brothers. He was such a kindhearted gentleman. He always called me Benjamin. We were so blessed to be able to work with him on that first album.

CeCe and I recorded our debut record in a small studio. I received all the affirmation that I needed during the recording process. When the producers smiled at me through the window, I got a sense that yeah, this was my future. I'd been looking through that soundproof glass my whole life. And that view, through the glass, was the future I wanted. It was a dream I had long before coming to PTL, and it was miraculous to see it come true. I remember holding our album in my hands for the first time. What a surreal feeling.

But with the good, there will be bad. And you must learn to deal with both. Of the other PTL Singers who weren't getting record deals, some were supportive, but I was a little suspicious of that support. They wanted to be part of our success without doing anything. We were strongly encouraged to remember that everyone at PTL— especially Jim—was a part of our record deal, even though CeCe and I were the only ones singing on it. Those feelings were due to the weird tension CeCe and I constantly lived in. I knew Jim was behind us—without a doubt. But when some of your closest friends find success, it's common to want to be related to that. So I chalked up the tension to that. But that doesn't mean I didn't feel it.

I knew that the record was *our* success, but we knew how to talk about it around the other PTL cast members and producers.

Our solution?

Gratitude.

Dad would have been proud.

We showed nothing but gratitude. All the while, we had a big secret in our back pockets: we wanted to leave PTL. The successful record revealed to us that our musical careers had other places to go. I didn't want to stay in Pineville my whole life. We were thankful. But no one could deny that we didn't exactly fit the mold at PTL.

PTL had reached outside its own boundaries in hiring us. Our diversity and enthusiasm may have helped PTL soar beyond its own expectations, but we knew that we needed to go beyond it. There were bigger things in our future.

BEGINNING TO FEEL THE DRIFT

When it was time for CeCe and me to promote our record, one stop was back home in Detroit. The atmosphere was electric in the theater when we performed in front of the people of our hometown. I didn't feel any of that awkwardness that I had tried so hard to shake in Pineville. It still crept up on me during some of the live PTL shows. But singing in Detroit was different. It felt right. It made me feel only more convinced that CeCe and I needed to leave.

But even though stepping onto a Detroit stage felt so comfortable, we were worried about Mom and Dad's re-action to our music. They had raised us singing a different kind of Gospel than we learned to sing at PTL. Many of the songs on our record had been in the secular market the first time that they were recorded. CeCe and I were singing about the Lord, though. We thought of our music as worship, and we sang it in praise of God. And that came through. We shouldn't have been worried about Mom. She absolutely loved our music, and Dad did too. Maybe Mom and Dad were able to hear "the Devil's music" differently when their son and daughter were singing it.

I knew that the other PTL Singers talked about us negatively while we were gone, the way that they had since we had gotten there. But I think that CeCe and I had started to win over some of the cast members. There was some dissension among the ranks, with some of the singers calling us proud and others calling those singers prejudiced. It was definitely time to make our exit. We didn't want our presence to sow discord in a place we weren't even going to stay.

We also knew that Jim and Tammy were clinging to us a little too tightly. It's that age-old problem. Someone starts thinking they might leave a place, and then the other people there cling to them too tightly. And all the clinging convinces the person that they have to get out—now. We walked back into that atmosphere not yet ready to tell Jim and Tammy that we were going to leave PTL and just jumped back into the routine of being two of the PTL Singers.

Things were changing, and I noticed some dissonance in our relationship with Jim. Jim was overjoyed at the continued success of PTL. He had his hotels and convention centers, and he had us. But he seemed to place much more value on our PTL success than on our record deal, which I suppose is natural when you run a business that happens to be a cable channel. We were interested in pursuing our record, but Jim didn't connect the dots very well. Whenever we tried to approach him about the path of our careers, he just kept telling us that he would continue to make us stars. And he truly wanted to—this we knew beyond a shadow of a doubt. But it's hard to balance your love and loyalty to a person while making a business decision about continuing to perform on the show. And that's what CeCe and I were attempting to do. We wanted to keep our relationship solid with Jim and Tammy, but we also wanted to do what was right for us, for our careers.

Life is chock-full of decisions like these. Knowing that doesn't make them any easier to make. But gaining the wisdom to deal with them begins with this kind of knowledge—that they're there and they're difficult. Somehow there's a settledness you feel when you know the decision is a hard one and there's no way but the hard way. Sometimes, you have to do what's right for you and your family and hope that the person across from you understands and continues to love you as a friend. That's what I was hoping for with Jim and Tammy.

CeCe and I, however, kept talking about these disconnects. Maybe CeCe and I were starting to understand that we were headed in different paths too. She loved to sing, but she didn't know if she wanted to make a whole career out of it. She knew exactly what I wanted, though. I wanted a career in music; I wanted to sing on big stages. In other words, I wanted the spotlight. I wanted to be a star.

The record, *Lord Lift Us Up,* was nominated for a Grammy. Our first nomination! I was twenty-one years old; CeCe was nineteen. The excitement, though, was short-lived. We were living our dream, but we didn't have our family's full support. Things in our family had been predetermined. We were to be part of the Winans Part Two. CeCe and I talked about our current situation with all the dreamy-eyed wonder you'd expect. But we knew things did not sit right with our family. As tight as our family was, that was a major concern.

Yet we still had to take advantage of the opportunity laid before us. We learned quickly that things don't always just slide right into place as you'd expect them to. With growth comes tension. Success brings good, but it also carries a weight. Starting with that first record with Bill, we began to feel the weight.

There was already a plan for me and for CeCe. We came from a family of singers. And the PTL Network was just a beginning. Once we had that experience under our belt, the idea held by my family members was that CeCe and I would return to Detroit and sing with the family.

Even before we left Detroit, we were already singing with them. So when we told the family about the opportunity for CeCe and me to record together as a duet, there were raised eyebrows.

Dad felt we had betrayed the original plan and we'd set out on our own, though that feeling eventually passed. Despite the unmet expectations at first, we always knew the family would support us. Well, *now* we know. Back then, it wasn't so clear. We were just overjoyed and amazed at our success off this one song. And we now had the chance to cut a record with Bill Maxwell, which was a dream come true.

We had to live in the tension of knowing that we'd hurt some family and the awesome reality of new opportunity.

We continued to sing for the show, but the record also needed to be supported. So we did the show during the week, and on the weekends, we sang at different churches and sometimes other venues. It was hard. We sang at more than three churches or venues on weekends, and Monday morning, we had to sound rested and be ready for whatever was on our schedule at PTL. But in addition to the grind of PTL and the new opportunities to sing out, other obstacles arose. One was learning how to connect with audiences.

CeCe and I didn't know how to do that. And to compound matters, CeCe is naturally shy. When it came time to speak from the stage in between songs or to welcome everybody, it was difficult for her.

Me, on the other hand? I wasn't a natural, but I had a very good teacher when it came to stage presence: Marvin. Marvin never worried about what people said or thought of him. He was comfortable in his own skin. He was the king of allowing yourself to relax and giving yourself permission to fail. That's how he was.

My dad was not good at remembering people's names at church, work, or play. Let's say Dad walked around church on a Sunday morning. Everyone was excited, all dressed up and milling around, getting their seats. And there came Robert. Dad would see Robert walking down the aisle, walk up to greet him, and say, "Hey, George, how are you? How are the kids?" Robert, whom my father has known for years, would look at him as though he were crazy, hurt by the fact that Dad didn't know his name, and walk away muttering to himself, "Oh my Lord, Dad Winans still does not remember my name."

But Dad did not care. He was unafraid to get someone's name wrong. People actually loved him for that. And I suppose some of that rubbed off on Marvin and me, or at least I'd like to think I learned from them.

I remember one night we were singing in Kansas City, and I said something like, "It's so good to be in Chicago tonight." CeCe whispered to me, "BeBe, we are in Kansas."

"Oh, OK," I replied. Followed by, "Good evening, Kansas!" And I'd just keep going on with the show. That was not an uncommon mistake for me. I'd flub, and roll with it, laugh at myself, and then sing my heart out.

We had to learn how to connect with audiences. How to relax. How to be ourselves. How to deal with the grind of performing and then working for the PTL Network.

There was no set path or guidebook for us to be able to do this well. And we probably didn't, but sometimes you just have to give it your best and allow yourself permission to learn as you go, to grow, and mold yourself into the best version of you.

Monday through Friday, we sang for *The PTL Club*, and that responsibility required us to rehearse. And not only the songs. We also had to rehearse singing in front of a camera, which was much different than singing in front of a live audience.

Part of that training required us to perform in a small room with a camera and a cameraman. And the camera didn't stay still. The cameramen moved up into our faces, and we had to learn to ignore the movement and keep our focus on the song and connecting with the audience on the other side of the camera.

Our instructors taught us to focus on nothing but the

camera. You have to envision the camera like a human being. It's another human being standing in front of you, watching you, and even though it's a machine, you have to learn to show emotion and connect with it. It basically taught us how to present a song and helped us get over any lingering fear of performing.

You can always tell when someone feels comfortable and knows how to connect through the camera, and I am thankful for that training. It really opened my eyes to a world within the world of entertainment I'd not known or experienced.

But all this talk about focus and performing reminds me of one of our live shows in which we all were challenged to stay focused. While some of us had to really concentrate, others apparently learned how to focus a little too well. Once we were singing with the ensemble on the show. And as we performed, a huge black fly flew all around us the entire time. That fly was so annoying!

But we had to remember our training. Keep singing. Focus on the camera. Nothing else matters. No matter what happens, just finish the song. Be professional!

Well, one of the women in our ensemble might have been a little too professional.

About halfway through the song, some of us noticed the fly was gone, and it wasn't until the song had ended and we were off the air that we found out the fate of the ugly big black fly.

She allowed that gross, big insect to fly right into her mouth!

I'm not lying.

She swallowed the monster bug and kept singing. She stayed focused. Remained professional!

CHAPTER THIRTEEN

JUST WHEN THINGS WERE GETTING GOOD

Whoever finds their life will lose it, and whoever loses their life for my sake will find it.

—Matthew 10:39

From the moment Jim and Tammy took us under their wing, everything seemed to get better and better. The show was a huge hit. The PTL Singers' first record sold off the charts. All our dreams were coming true.

But in 1983, everything began to change.

It all started with an announcement CeCe made to each of us individually, and then to the family as a whole, at the age of nineteen.

"I'm getting married."

I was shocked, and so was the family, except my two

137

other sisters, Angelique and Debra, who were fifteen and twelve at the time, respectively, who were not affected by CeCe's decision.

This was so shocking to hear because CeCe was not the dating kind. Growing up, she didn't show a lot of interest in boys. She was more focused on heavenly things. This announcement blindsided us. No one saw it coming.

Alvin Love. Yes, the brother-in-law-to-be had the last name Love. Can you imagine how much love flowed from our hearts?

I racked my brain but could not figure out where this marriage talk was coming from. When did she even meet Alvin? CeCe and I were still living in Charlotte, North Carolina, but with success we could afford to visit our home in Detroit more often. And it was during one of those visits that our brother Ronald introduced CeCe to Alvin. The introduction I can't remember. Alvin came down to visit us in Charlotte, and what went on between the two of them is lost in my memory.

At the Sunday service in Charlotte, before Jim preached his sermon, CeCe told me she was going to marry Alvin. I told her right then and there that I was not attending her wedding. I also told her how her decision was selfish and the biggest mistake of her life.

The whole family felt that the dating process was too short for CeCe to really know Alvin. Add in the long-distance relationship. Yes, distance makes the heart grow fond, but distance also leads to good behavior when you finally see each other face-to-face. And what you get is your best self with the person's best self. There's really no time to confess your other side, that other side we keep hidden, that other side that only time can reveal, that other side that completes the picture of the other person and allows us to make a more informed choice.

The age gap between Alvin and CeCe was seventeen years! He was the ripe old age of thirty-six.

I want to be fair. Was there anything about him that should have caused CeCe to second-guess herself, to make her think she was making a horrible decision? No. But what was clear to me at the age of twenty-one was that if she went with her heart and did marry Alvin, life for the both us would change drastically. That's why I thought her decision marked the worst day of my life and our career, which had just left the runway.

Priscilla Marie Winans, which is her full name, had drawn a line in the sand, and no matter what Daddy or Momma said, her mind was made up and couldn't be changed. And CeCe had some firepower when her age was questioned. She could remind my mother that she had been only seventeen years old when she said, "I do," to my father. And Dad was CeCe's age, nineteen! They were babies in love and babies in marriage! For the most part my mom and dad had a great marriage.

My mother at the age of twenty-five had already given

birth to seven boys! The thought causes me to still buckle at the knees. It also caused my mom and dad to work multiple jobs in order to make ends meet, to pay the bills, feed, and clothe us. No easy feat, but they did it.

One thing Alvin had going for him was his employment at the Broadcast Music Incorporated (BMI). He was a handsome fella and seemingly mild mannered. But was this the facade to keep us away from learning and knowing the real Alvin that the eyes couldn't see?

Why was he still single? Was he once married and now divorced and not sharing that information with CeCe or our family? If this was not the case, then why would he want to marry a teenager? These were questions raised by the Winans family; CeCe was not budging.

During that church service when I told CeCe I was not coming to her wedding, I knew it was an awful thing to say. I knew I broke her heart. But CeCe and I were close not only in age but in life. My father taught us that we were responsible for each other. Was I my sister's keeper? Yes! According to my dad, when one of us was down, all of us were down; and when one Winans wins, all Winanses win.

CeCe and I went to elementary school together and even graduated from high school together. CeCe graduated two years earlier than expected because she didn't want to be in school without me; at least I believe that's why she did it. Even in high school we shared lockers and classes together. Some even thought we were not really brother and sister because we had fun being together, which wasn't reality for a lot of other siblings. When I said I wasn't attending the most important event of her life, it struck her in her heart.

Then Pastor Jim Bakker took to the pulpit and preached about love. When he concluded the sermon on the true definition of love, I turned to CeCe and said, "I'm coming to your wedding."

My heart was conflicted, but beside all my doubts and fears and anger, love had just trumped them all.

CeCe, with tears running down her face and giving God praise as she always did, then asked, "BeBe, will you sing at the wedding?"

My answer?

"Don't get ahead of God. I'm just coming."

There were moments in my early career when I just felt like this whole thing was not going to work out. And when those times emerged, my mother and father were there to keep me from giving up those dreams. They also put me in my place when I wanted God to blot out the day Ronald introduced CeCe and Alvin.

In those situations, God helped me understand what faith really is. Faith is all those moments in which we are not in control of what's happening. Those moments when life is not working out how we planned. In those moments, I learned that I need to stop leaning on my own understanding and accept, by faith, that God's plan was at work.

The other question was: "If CeCe really goes through with this, where will they live? Alvin is employed at a great company, which happens to be in Detroit, not Charlotte. Oh my Lord, she's going to leave me and all that is happening for us in North Carolina and move back to Motor City Detroit! And then, they will start having kids right away, if, for no other reason, so that Alvin can enjoy them and grow older with them." (In my eyes, he was already old.)

CeCe's marriage meant the end. CeCe and I would have to break the news to Jim and Tammy. How and when would have to be carefully thought out and well executed.

TIME FOR YOU TO LEAVE

My conversations with CeCe followed a pattern. I was convinced that her marriage meant abandonment—of me, of our dreams, of everything we'd worked so hard to achieve. She insisted that it meant none of those things. I struggled to believe her. I struggled to understand why God would lead us to Pineville, open me up to the possibility of a successful career as a singer—something I dreamed about my entire life—only to have it swept away with two words: "I do."

CeCe understood my frustration, and she shared my love

for what God was doing with our careers. She also told me about her dreams to build her own life, with a family. She believed she could pursue building a family while she was building her career as a singer with me. She promised that she was not giving up on "BeBe and CeCe," but she admitted that she might have to leave PTL.

To me, they were one and the same. I couldn't separate them like she could, and it made me angry. I felt she was abandoning everything we worked for and was thinking only about herself. I had to find peace and release my fears and let her pursue her true love and what she wanted.

I learned the bond between brothers and sisters is strange. It's almost as though the years of shared experiences and countless memories allow you to say the worst possible things to one another, knowing deep down that the love you share will eventually cover over the hurt you feel. It's the only way to explain why, after all that CeCe and I had been through together, I could look at her teary eyes and stay stone-faced and silent while she pleaded with me. My words were not right, but we do tend to hurt the ones we love with the deepest blows.

I'm sure we prayed different prayers. Her prayers probably asked God to change my mind and to help me see more clearly that this was exactly what was planned before the foundations of the world and that in no time Alvin and I would bond like twin brothers. Mine were not so Christian, asking God to send an alien from Mars to kidnap Alvin and wipe our memories that Alvin ever existed on Earth.

I can still hear that simple message Jim preached about love. The question he asked us that day was, "How do you love God, whom you cannot see, and not love your brother, whom you can see?" I felt those words lodge in my heart and a lump rise in my throat.

"It's a gift!" Jim lifted his hands. "God loves us despite all the things we do wrong, whether we agree or not."

His words faded into a blur with the organ music behind him, as the Scripture rang in my ears. How do you love God, whom you cannot see, and not love your brother...or sister...whom you can see? The answer to that question is simply: you can't.

I am glad that I allowed God's words in that moment to cut me deep and cause me to look down at CeCe and see the little girl I used to share a church pew with, the little girl who shared classrooms with me, who substituted Vaseline for lip gloss, the little girl with a dream in her heart, the same dream as I had in mine.

I cleared my throat and whispered, "I'll be at your wedding."

I wrote a song for the celebration entitled "I'm Gonna Miss You." I sang it with my brothers as CeCe walked down the aisle to meet Mr. Love.

CHAPTER FOURTEEN

LETTING IT GO

"For my thoughts are not your thoughts,
neither are your ways my ways,"
declares the LORD.

—Isaiah 55:8

CeCe's marriage was one of those things that I just learned to accept. It wasn't too hard, because she seemed to be really happy with Alvin. There were still some hurt feelings about keeping the relationship a secret, but all in all I understood. There were other things that were more difficult to accept. The Lord must have been trying to teach me something about acceptance during that time.

I had to accept that I was from Detroit, but I lived in

Pineville, and that I felt like I was from two worlds that couldn't be connected. I learned to accept that my role on PTL was still relatively small when I looked at the record business as a whole. I learned to accept that black people would always be the minority on PTL, and I learned to accept the silent criticism of the other singers. I had to learn to accept the things in life I couldn't control. I had to let it go.

They never said anything directly to our faces, but some were jealous of us, there was no doubt of that. Jim and Tammy loved us, and they promoted us fearlessly. We were in the spotlight all the time. The other guys said that Jim and Tammy promoted us and thrust us into the spotlight because we were black, despite the fact that we were considered two of the best singers on the show. And everybody knew it. We had changed their look, enlivened their style, and broadened their audience. We were the cause of the spike in *The PTL Show*'s ratings, so we were more profitable than the other singers on the show. I had come a long way from being a grocery boy who sang only in the Sunday choir, and CeCe was more popular with the viewers than any other female performer.

Still, CeCe and I were careful not to let pride take over even with all the attention and with a pay raise. I struggled with my own pride, but I never said anything to Jim and Tammy's other singers. The burden was on me to be the bigger man. This wasn't just because of my belief in the Gospel message and in turning the other cheek. The reality was that they could get away with meanness that I couldn't because they were white and I was black. That I was black mattered more to them than my character, and it was one of those things that I've spent my whole life learning to accept.

END IT OR SHE'S FIRED

I remember one difficult conversation with Tammy that encapsulates what I'm saying. Once, Tammy confronted a close friend of mine named Penny, after CeCe had moved to Detroit and I was still living in Charlotte. The confrontation was about her relationship with me. Penny was Jim's makeup artist. And a white woman.

Penny, CeCe, and I were friends. She had been kind to us even before CeCe and I became star talents on the show. We were close. We ate together. We went to movies together. We did everything together. We were always together. There was a true friendship between the three of us.

But the optics weren't good, I suppose, which prompted Tammy to approach Penny. She told Penny that her relationship with me had to end. It was OK when it was CeCe, Penny, and I hanging out together. But after CeCe had left, and Penny and I were seen everywhere together, people started to whisper and assumed we were dating, which I found out was a no-no in the Christian world of Pineville.

But Penny did not back down.

"Tammy, you can't tell me who I can and cannot be friends with."

Tammy fired Penny for refusing to dial back the relationship. That same day, Penny showed up at my door crying.

"What's wrong?" I asked.

"She fired me."

"Who fired you?"

"They fired me. She fired me."

"Who fired you?"

"Tammy!" said Penny. "She told me that we could not hang out anymore, but I told her she couldn't tell me who I could be friends with, so she fired me."

I couldn't believe my ears. So right then and there, I said, "Well, if that's the way of it, then let's give them something to talk about."

Penny and I started dating. The only reason I ended it was because of all the drama of us being together in the South and the tension and heartache it caused. I knew that I could not go the rest of my life with the kind of scrutiny and tension it caused because not only was the white Christian community upset by it, it was not approved in the black community either. Especially with black women. When they saw me with Penny or when they heard I was dating a white woman, the remarks were, "Oh, so we're not good enough for you?" I understand those comments now a little more, but I believe love is love and God is the judge.

The ordeal opened me up to the inside world of Christianity. I saw the politics, the power struggle.

WHO'S READY FOR POPS WINANS?

Jim and Tammy were riding high on the wave of their recent success. The high ratings produced bigger paychecks, and they started to diversify their PTL venture. They were opening hotels left and right. They were bringing everybody to Pineville to worship the Lord together. It was a kind of Christian entertainment that people had never even heard of or dreamed about. They opened an amusement park—Heritage USA. I didn't understand what waterslides had to do with worship, but I figured that we might as well enjoy everything that our "white parents" could dream up, even if we never would have thought of it ourselves.

And then Jim and Tammy did something we never expected, something much further in the outfield than waterslides. They invited Dad on the show to sing live. Jim and Tammy were so excited about it. When they told us that they were going to ask him, I just nodded. I couldn't stop them, and I didn't think that I should. I knew he would come down. Our parents missed us, no matter what they said, and they were sacrificing for us to have this opportunity.

I also knew that Jim and Tammy were taking on more than they bargained for with Dad. I think they were expecting an older version of me. I had been singing for Jim and Tammy, in front of their audience. And I was trained how to connect with that audience. That kind of training can change you. I sounded different after a few years in Pineville.

But Dad was untainted by Pineville. I'd been listening to Dad sing since I was born, and I knew his style. I knew how he'd sound to those white Southern people. Dad was all Detroit Gospel. And in Detroit, the chorus could go on as long as the Spirit led. What they got with Dad was God's honest truth of Gospel.

The day came for Dad's big premiere on PTL. CeCe and I warmed up the crowd as best we could, but we knew that it wouldn't be enough to make what Dad was going to do look "normal" to any of the people in our audience or in our Sunday choir. Jim told the audience that there was going to be a special blessing on today's showing of PTL. Jim and Tammy knew their audience loved us, so why wouldn't they love Pop? Jim introduced "Pop Winans" enthusiastically, and Dad took the center of the stage. Dad started with the version of "I Got a New Home" that everyone had rehearsed. But after a few verses, Dad got away from everybody, including us.

I'll never forget what those PTL Singers looked like while they were watching Dad sing. He swayed perfectly in time with the music, even as the tempo accelerated. His eyes were closed, and sweat beaded on his forehead. And he just didn't stop—he didn't stop until he was finished. He repeated the same chorus over and over, caught up completely in praising the Lord. He believed that Zion was his new home; he believed it with his whole body. And some of those PTL people were so taken aback, they just stood there with their mouths open. Dad finished the song on his own.

Pineville people weren't used to singing like that. They knew that he was talented, they knew that he was singing to the Lord, but they were frozen. They couldn't join in worship like Dad's; it was too raw, too real. Maybe too black. Even Jim and Tammy were stunned. Jim led the studio audience in tentative applause, and Dad shuffled backstage. He didn't have it in him to be embarrassed, and I was glad. He'd always cared more about the Lord's approval than the approval of the audience.

I have pictures in my head of Dad bent over onstage, his eyes closed, gripping the microphone and singing as if the power of his voice could usher in the Holy Spirit himself. The sweat, the pure soul that would almost rage into the microphone and then out into the audience: it was a sight to behold, and a sound by which to be enraptured. And when he sang with Mom, she'd hang by him, swaying with the music, caught up in it too, listening to Dad and waiting for the heavens to open.

This kind of almost naked singing—the kind where you bare all on the stage regardless of what the audience was thinking or feeling—this was pure Detroit Gospel, but also pure Pops Winans. It wasn't canned. It wasn't manufactured. It was from the very gut of Dad. And when you bare your guts onstage, people sometimes don't know what to do with that. Well, *white people* sometimes don't know what to do with that. It wakes up your soul and brings life to your bones.

It's this kind of nakedness that becomes popular and can even catapult someone to fame even though, ironically, it cares nothing about name-making. When you forget about fame and you allow the worship moment to grip you, God listens. And God loves. I can see Him joining in with someone like Dad, who, like David danced naked before the Lord, sings, baring his entire being on the stage.

CeCe and I knew that he'd taken it too far for Pineville, but I was proud of him. I was proud of him even though I knew that the PTL Singers weren't the only ones who couldn't join in with him—people everywhere changed the channel on Dad's Detroit Gospel. Pop didn't care about ratings, but that the episode may not have lived up to Jim and Tammy's usual standard.

After Dad came on the show, the scorn from the same jealous singers got worse. Dad's performance was like a big reminder that CeCe and I were different. We were from a different place, Dad's place, and we sang differently. No amount of Bakker favoritism could change that. Some of them started confronting Jim and Tammy directly, wanting to know if they had any more Winans-related surprises like Dad up their sleeves. PTL wasn't a comfortable place for those guys anymore, but they stuck around anyway. They thought their stubbornness would somehow get PTL to go back to the way it used to be. They liked us. But more black people—other black people—that would be too much.

Tammy defended all of us, of course. She was more surprised than I was by the overt racism of the PTL crew. She must have thought that since she and Jim accepted us, everybody else would too. She wanted her example to somehow eliminate the hate in everyone's hearts. But the acceptance of a few people can lead to even more hate on the part of everyone else. It starts a fire. Tammy didn't know this, but I did.

Jim dressed down anyone who thought of black people as different and told them that they needed to pray. He knew that prayer could not pray their hate away, but it was and is still the place to start. Tammy took a bit of a harsher approach—she threatened to fire anyone who brought up the topic of me, CeCe, and our involvement with PTL. She put quite a few of the other singers on the "naughty list." They'd lose privileges for calling us derogatory names around Tammy, even once. People started getting uninvited to nice meals and events. The Bakker posse was dwindling. And even though Tammy didn't mean for this to happen, we looked more like her favorites than ever. Just something else I'd have to accept.

I can't control how people react to me. I suppose there was a time I tried to or wanted to. But those efforts quickly proved futile. I learned that success can bring comparison and competition. People want to be like you, they want to be better than you, they want to replace you. That comes with the territory.

But there are other situations that have nothing to do with success. People don't want to be like you, they want to destroy you. I learned that a few years after being at PTL. I'd begun to cope with the comparison and competition, but nothing could prepare me for the words Rick spoke to me one day after I prayed with him.

CHAPTER FIFTEEN

TEACHING LOVE INSTEAD OF HATE

No one is born hating another person because of the color of his skin, or his background, or his religion. People must learn to hate, and if they can learn to hate, they can be taught to love, for love comes more naturally to the human heart than its opposite.

—Nelson Mandela, *Long Walk to Freedom*

"I hated you."

"What?" I replied.

"I hated you," he said through tears. "Day after day you came to me, placed your hand on my shoulder, and told me you were praying for my wife. I didn't know how to respond."

"What do you mean, respond?"

"My parents taught me to hate black people. That's how I grew up. And when you told me you were praying for me and my wife to not suffer another miscarriage, it broke me. I was taught hate, when I should have been taught how to love."

Rick worked the camera at PTL the entire time my sister and I sang on the show. I saw him every day. And when I heard about his wife's pregnancy, I was excited, but what I didn't know was the history they had suffered with all her pregnancies ending in miscarriages. I wanted him to know that I was praying for our God to show Himself faithful and that He would give them the desires of their hearts. And that's what God did! That's what my parents taught me to do. To pray for people who needed help from a loving God.

There is no color boundary or socioeconomic boundary for prayer. Everyone deserves to be prayed for. Which is really just another way to say that everyone needs to be loved.

When I joined the show with CeCe, we were just kids. When I think back on those years, it's hard to believe we did what we did at such a young age and that our parents let us. But who would have thought that these two black kids from Detroit could have such an impact? It's just another reminder that God can use anyone at any time, any age.

Rick was thirty-seven and grew up in the South, and there was a long history of prejudice in his family. But our presence there and just caring about others helped to change Rick's heart. In that instance I learned one of the greatest lessons a person can learn in life: love is more powerful than hate.

Love is a gift. And I think for some people it comes more naturally than others. For me, it's natural. I love people. I probably get that characteristic from my mother. But like any gift we're born with, if you don't use it, if it lays dormant, it gets tough to use. I believe you and me, we're born to love one another. Who could ever imagine a world in which we were born to hate?

But think about it. When we don't use our gift of love, what replaces it? Hate. It's easy to hate. It's difficult to love. And since hatred is easy, we practice it more. If I hadn't used my gift all the years before that, I'm sure my reaction to Rick would have been different. I have my family to thank for that.

Rick hugged me and, in tears, asked for forgiveness. He was thankful. Why? Because not only did he and his wife have a beautiful child, but the chains of hatred in his heart had been broken.

There are reasons why people hate. Some people are raised in cultures of hatred and prejudice. It's systemic. And it takes brave souls to end it. The choice I made in that moment was to love Rick, to forgive him. It wasn't

157

easy, but it was something ingrained in me—maybe that made it feel more natural.

When Rick confessed his hatred, I remembered what my mother used to say when I'd fight with my brother. "That's your brother," she'd say. "You love your brother. You apologize to him. We listen to each other because we love each other."

We listen because we love.

How would our world look right this moment, in the media, on the internet, in our homes, in our communities, in our politics, if we employed this bit of wisdom from my mother? When we listen to one another, we pay attention to one another and, as the dictionary says, we "make an effort to hear something." And there's that hard word: effort. Hate requires little effort. It doesn't require us to listen. Rather, it encourages us to react—and often without thinking.

I remember sitting in the audience listening to professor and author Tony Campolo once. He explained how he always had a constant flow of young people coming to his office. "It wasn't because of anything I did," he said, "only that I listened."

I'm not perfect when it comes to listening. We all stumble at times in our pride. But if we can just put forth the effort to listen to one another, if we can just take the time to hear another person's story, it's within our reach to be people of love rather than people of hate.

Even when it's hard. Even in the face of blatant racism. Even in the face of stark sexism. Even in the face of religious persecution. We can still listen. We can still love.

For me, listening and loving have been lifelong pursuits. Not something I learned in a moment. But it is something I was born into. So I've spent my entire life pursuing. In such a pursuit, a person never arrives, but I've found it's the perseverance of journey that makes all the difference. The more time we spend loving others, listening to their stories, the more empathetic we become, the more loving we become. That same principle applies to forgiveness.

LEARNING TO FORGIVE

Martin Luther King Jr. said, "Forgiveness is not an occasional act; it is a permanent attitude."[11] That's a tough thing to live out. How can you and I keep a constant attitude of forgiveness?

One of my nephews once asked my dad what he wanted his legacy to be. My dad responded, "To be a man who forgave—everybody." That's a tall order. But it's an excellent goal to live by. Rick lived for thirty-seven years and kept his bias covered up. And it wasn't until someone showed him some compassion that he was able to confront his own prejudice. I hate to think about what might have happened if I'd acted like a jerk to him, or was insensitive, or held it over him.

Having love ingrained in my soul by my parents, I was able to show forgiveness. Interesting how when we listen and love, forgiveness seems like an obvious thing to give people. But when hate becomes our first response, we hold grudges and division follows.

Forgiveness is a powerful tool.

But honestly, when Rick first said that he had hated me, I didn't know how to take it. Thinking back, I remember feeling as though he had deceived me all that time. He was close to me. He filmed me for years. But in the moment that he revealed he hated me, something happened inside me. I learned, after my initial shock, that love is greater than hatred. Rick said, "You loved me, and I'm so embarrassed and feel so bad for keeping those hateful thoughts inside me. But I saw how you loved me by praying for me, and it broke me."

This experience opened me up to a world I did not see. I had to process it. It really wasn't his fault. His parents, whom he loved, seemed to have taught him to hate. Mine, whom I loved, taught me to love. How can I hate this person who had to grow in and through his prejudices?

Later in my career I rolled up to a very nice restaurant in L.A. I'd already had my car valeted, and after my expensive meal I was standing outside waiting for my car to arrive. While I waited, a white man and his beautiful wife and family pulled up in a convertible. He stepped out of his car and said, "Here you go," holding out his keys, not even really seeing me. I was so confused, because I enjoy fashion, and in both casual and formal outings, I never look like I'm working a valet lot.

"Oh, son," I thought to myself.

There I stood, a black man in front of a fine-dining restaurant and this white man thought I was the valet. I could have given him a piece of my mind. Or I could keep my composure and not say anything. Maybe he was like Rick and grew up with parents and relatives who taught him that all black people work in such jobs. Whatever *his* background, I'm responsible for *me* and *my* response. And in that moment, I chose love. I chose to forgive. "I'm waiting for the valet to bring my car too. I hope your meal is as delicious as the one I just finished here at this fabulous restaurant," I replied.

Rick's response to my praying for him collects the whole experience of moving from Detroit to Charlotte in a tight little scene in which love breaks through hate. I still run into folks like Rick. But as a young man who was basically thrown into the world of white Southern Christianity, this encounter signaled the beginning of

161

perspective changing, expanding, and the reality of the world settling in.

It was in this context that I cut my teeth as a professional musician. I could've taken the easy road and left Charlotte for safer, more familiar surroundings. My heart longed for Detroit all the time. In Detroit, I would have been comfortable. In your own surroundings, you know what parts of town to stay away from; you know, that part of town you don't go to when it's dark. All my friends from school were in Detroit. And most of them were black. And church? The same thing. My life in Detroit was predominantly a black experience.

Did I experience racism in Detroit? Yes, but not in my face, or in our churches and schools. Ms. Byers was one of my favorite teachers, and Ms. McKowskie too. They were white, and we loved them. Ms. Byers introduced me to poetry. Her class was instrumental in guiding me to write songs that were poetic.

But I just felt that God had a plan, and that it was for this moment I was born.

Rick's experience was my first time encountering blatant racism. It was the first time racism came to the forefront and I really saw it. Before, I had heard about it from others. But nothing's "real" until you experience it yourself. I'd read books about it. But it was never right in front of me personally. Was I prepared for racism within the walls of Christ? That was very difficult to accept and deal with. You did say you loved God. How can you hate your brother in that way? That was the disconnect for me, as I'd like to think it would have been for anyone.

RACISM IS TAUGHT

I'm blessed when I look back on my foundation. Those who brought us up in church showed us love by example, a priceless foundation. And it still helps me to weather the storm, to deal with people who didn't have that foundation.

I've learned that racism is taught. We were taught to love everybody. We were taught that God's love is for everyone. That was my view of God and my foundation of love. When I was introduced to something different, it challenged me to make a decision on what I was taught. Was I taught the truth? Or was there something I was missing?

What about looking for a way to react? I had a choice to either love or to hate. I chose love because my foundation was built on love. Why do some choose hate? Because they're taught that. I feel anger at times when I am treated unfairly, but how I react when I am treated poorly comes down to choices. We can react on our feelings and not regret it. No remorse. But that is a toxic choice. Hatred will eat remorse away from you. It will remove your common sense. It will chip at everything humane about you. Proverbs 26:5 says, "Answer a fool according to his folly, or he will be wise in his own eyes." Don't waste too much time with haters; they are fools. We must all choose how to respond when confronted with hate. Our country has a long way to go with regard to how minorities are treated.

CHAPTER SIXTEEN

THE LONELINESS OF FAME

It is not good to eat much honey,
nor is it glorious to seek one's own glory.

—Proverbs 25:27 (ESV)

My life was full of contradictions. I was starting to be successful, but at times I was lonely. Sometimes I'd tell myself, "Maybe it's time to fall in love, BeBe. Settle down like CeCe did when she found Alvin." But I knew in time that would happen. One of the reasons for my loneliness was that I was continually around the other PTL Singers, who were all white. Their friends were white too. Interracial dating was still frowned upon. The societal pressure wasn't the only reason, but there it was. The contrast of my race against the majority race of Pineville affected me every day—evidence of my contradictory existence.

At the same time, I was also feeling more successful than I had ever been in my life. My dream of working hard and singing finally seemed to be coming true. I wasn't naive to the effects of fame. I'd observed them in close proximity growing up. I also witnessed them in my brothers' lives.

In our culture, just about everyone wants their moment of fame. But seeing, understanding, and dealing with it when you get a taste of it are all different things. When you're twenty-something, and you watch singers and bands and actors become famous, that's all you want. The pinnacle is to be known, to be seen.

It's not until you reach the other side of the stage that you recognize the steep price of fame. CeCe and I weren't mega-famous. But fame comes in all shapes and sizes. Fame is like a drug. You shoot it up, you smoke it, and you have to have it; then when it has you in its grip it reveals to you its vast emptiness.

People think you have it all.

"Look, he's up there on TV, singing. He must be living it up," they say.

"He must go home to all sorts of people who love him," they think.

When the truth is, I was still very much out of my element. I was enjoying the affection, and I was doing what I loved, but I was still just a young man. I wanted real friends who weren't singing with me on television. That's when Detroit would rise up in my brain. I'd miss it. I'd miss my family. I still loved spreading my wings, and it was good to be away, but when things get hard, you want a piece of home. You want to walk home and be one of the Winans kids again.

Dealing with fame wasn't just about being lonely sometimes and wishing to be home with my family. It was about the pursuit of being known. Not only did I have the real-life struggle of popularity, but I also wrestled with the tension of whether it was even a good thing. My upbringing, great as it was, drilled certain virtues into me. And one of those virtues was humility.

A world like ours that thirsts for fame doesn't give many pointers for pursuing humility. That's something you put into play when you're thanking the world for awards, right? "I want to thank God and my family for keeping me humble and focused," et cetera.

It always cracks me up when I watch interviews with sports figures after a big win. During the game, when they score a touchdown or dunk a basketball, they gallivant all over the place, pointing at their names on their jerseys or doing some self-indulgent dance. Then they stand before the press, with their serious faces, and say, "We just need to stay focused, and humble, and get another win."

If the world teaches us anything, it's how to draw

attention to ourselves. It's not a bad thing to perform in front of people, whether it's as an athlete, singer, politician, or pastor. Being on a stage doesn't make you a bad person. It's what you do with that stage that makes all the difference.

Once I was asked to attend an awards ceremony and then sing at the after party in Beverly Hills—the swankiest of places. Everyone you'd want to see was there. I was impressed with the crowd and the place and was thankful for the invitation. But as soon as I was finished performing, I walked off the stage and went back to my hotel room to go to bed. If there's one thing I've learned all these years, it's that I need sleep. I don't need to see and be seen at late-night events. I don't do crazy, risky things. To me, that's not what it means to be famous.

WHAT IT MEANS TO BE FAMOUS

I heard a famous athlete once say that he didn't sign up to be a role model; he just wanted to play sports and become rich and famous. In my younger days I probably would have agreed with him. But my definition of being famous shifted, matured. Being famous is an opportunity to become a better version of yourself, and model that version to young people and old people alike. But most important, to model who you are to God first and then to yourself.

Here's what I mean by being a role model to God and to yourself: being a role model to God means living up to the potential He put inside you. It means living with integrity and virtue. It means being accountable for what you say and being unashamed to admit when you're wrong. Every role model needs to be able to say, "I was wrong. I'm sorry. Will you forgive me?"

Whether you're known across the seas or across the street, we are all famous in that there is always someone looking up to us, trying to model themselves after us, whether good or bad.

I believe also with fame we become mirrors to other people. They look at us, and they see how we dress, how we walk and talk, where we live. They look at us, and they see themselves or what they think they want to be. That is a huge responsibility. In all I do, my main goal is to be the best mirror I can be for those who are looking at me as an example for how to look and talk and be. We all need to strive to be the best mirrors we can be, and we need to bring honesty along for the ride.

Being famous also entails overcoming our mistakes. Mistakes are a part of our journey, and without them there is no need for correction. God gave His Son because of our mistakes, and through the gift of His Son's life, I can leave my mistakes in the past, both present and future mistakes. Pros and cons meet me on every level, and the more I become disciplined, the better I become a role model. "Discipline." That can be a tough word. But it doesn't have to be.

Recently I told someone that I'm now choosing to define the word "discipline" as something positive, not the negative idea of discipline I learned when I was young. Whenever I heard someone, or even the Word of God, use the word "discipline," I felt as though something was being demanded of me. Driven into me. In the Bible it does say that when you love someone, like your children, you will discipline them. And it says that God disciplines His children like a parent does. But it is only for a short time, and it doesn't mean that He's constantly bending us over His knee.

Now that I'm older, I understand that discipline is a very good thing. And becoming disciplined takes a lifetime; it takes determination and patience. It takes patience to achieve anything of lasting value in this world. At this stage of my life, the most important person I want to please, the most important person whom I want to be known by, is Jesus. I want us to be close. I want Him to be my role model, and what a role model He is, and yes, He's famous.

DISSONANCE

There seemed to be dissonance at every turn. In our relationship with Jim and Tammy, in our relationships with the other singers on the show, and there was the dissonance I always struggled with: wanting the same opportunities that others had so that I could display my talent on the big stage and still live a Christian life. The Christian life is a life of self-sacrifice, of becoming less, of bearing your cross. Could I be a Christian and still pursue the big stage?

It's tormenting to have a dream and feel as though you can't love Jesus if you achieve that dream. That sounds stupid to my ears now. But not back then. Sure, I grew up in Detroit, the land of superstar singers, but there was this underlying notion in the church that if you were doing anything successful, it was worldly.

You should only be inspired to do things for the Lord. If it's outside of that, it's worldly. Forget fashion. Forget being a judge or going to school to become a doctor. We didn't have time for those pursuits. We had to attend revival.

Where I grew up, if you became successful—and I mean just found some success, not even fame, just success— people thought you'd done something worldly. Because fame is not of God. It's not what church is about. But that's a lie.

Now I see it more clearly. We didn't have balance. Jesus doesn't want you and me sitting around in churches all day long only doing things that relate to it. He created this beautiful world so that we could enjoy it, find our place in it, and work hard at what were gifted in. He takes joy in seeing us use our gifts for His Kingdom. He loves when you dance, or preach, or teach, or landscape houses. He loves when I sing, and I know that He does because I can feel that heavenly joy in the deepest part of my being when I sing onstage. I can almost hear Him whisper, "BeBe, yes, BeBe. You were born for this, my son! Now get soulful with it!"

At other times I can imagine Him saying, "What are y'all doing? I'm concerned about every aspect of your life. I'm concerned about how you feel, what you love, and the big dreams you have."

Think about God when He spoke to His people. He spoke to them in dreams. But forget your dreams. We can love God, the God who does the miraculous, yet we can't dream about becoming what we feel in our hearts is right to do? That's crazy to me. Back then, though, it created a heavy tension in my life. And it almost paralyzed me.

If it were not for the voices of my mother and father, of Howard and Marvin, or Ronald and CeCe, of good friends like Jim and Tammy, Margaret Bell, Harry Dawkins, Whitney Houston, and others who are not household names, I may still be somewhere still struggling with it. But thank you Jesus, I had and still have friends like them. Friends who know me better than I know myself. Friends who love me and want me to use my voice for God's glory. Friends who know that I can still sing for God's glory on a big stage in front of lights on television.

A friend told me this once: being famous with God is the best kind of fame. How can someone be famous before God? That seems impossible and even wrong. But the idea of being famous before God means that He cares for you, and you matter to Him. Being famous before God sounds like Him telling me, "BeBe, you're OK. I love you. Now, do what I've gifted you to do."

It's humbling to think about God running after me as my Father and friend. With all my shortcomings and screw-ups, He still loves me.

Fame can be lonely, the pursuit of fame even lonelier. But where fame has its blessings, they are only temporary. And if you're not careful, it can rule you and take you over—it can seize your heart and never let go. But the grip of God's love on you is what I want.

I'm thankful for that young man who struggled with loneliness, and with fitting in, and with the tension of pursuing success and fame. He had a lot of help and wisdom given to him along the way. And if I can be that help to you, then that fills me with joy. Joy wins over fame.

CHAPTER SEVENTEEN

LEAVING THE PTL

In all your ways submit to him,
and he will make your paths straight.

—Proverbs 3:6

It took Ronald, that constant voice of support for me and CeCe, some time before he was able to come down south and watch us sing on the PTL and witness the life that we had made for ourselves. When he finally did make the trip, I showed him around. I took him to a few of my favorite Pineville spots, and he sat in on a recording of the show and some of our performances. He joked with me and brought me some of the news from the family.

Visiting with him reminded me that, above all, I was

175

still a Winans brother. Ronald didn't care that we had spent our last few years away from the family. He knew that Mom and Dad had sent us down to Pineville so we could explore our dreams of singing. Sometimes you have to let go of people in order to give them what they need. And anyway, family was stronger than location. And family knows what we need better than anyone else, with the exception of the Lord. But I've found that the two work in tandem. The Lord will use one of my family members to tell me what I need to hear the most.

During Ronald's Pineville visit, he was able to tell me what I needed to hear. During a quiet moment backstage before one of our performances, I took the time to share some of my troubles with him—about the tension and the competition. Ronald was wise, kind with a little bit of sarcasm, and, most important, honest with me.

He already knew that CeCe had made her mind up to leave PTL, and I decided if she left that I would leave too. But I was still worried about that decision. I was hesitant and wondered if I was making the right decision. With Ronald I could let the words spill out, no matter how raw or messy. I knew he would give me an honest answer. He knew we were not being ungrateful or foolhardy. Actually, Ronald wasn't surprised at all. He took it in stride, just like he took everything else. I told him that we just hadn't been able to tell the Bakkers yet. This didn't surprise him either.

Ronald reminded me of the similar situation that my brothers had to deal with when Marvin was feeling the call to ministry and how it wasn't easy for Marvin to tell the others that he'd have to leave the group for a while and go after this calling with all his heart, mind, and soul. He resonated with the way Marvin was feeling and how it took courage to tell the others. In time, they all understood. I could resonate with that, too. He didn't want to hurt them, just like CeCe and I didn't want to hurt the Bakkers.

Then Ronald gave me some real wisdom. He told me that both sides were going to struggle but that change was inevitable. With time comes understanding of God's perfect plans for our future—plans we can't see. I'm almost sure that Marvin also struggled with leaving; worrying how the brothers would feel. Maybe I was doing the same thing. I wanted to leave PTL, yes, but maybe I was just worried that I was going to fail out there in the big world. At the very least, PTL offered us a certain amount of comfort. We were *known,* and we had an audience for the foreseeable future. I needed more courage to finally cut ties with PTL.

I also confided in Ronald that I'd been writing some songs. Late into the night, after PTL recordings and rehearsals were over, I was scratching lyrics into one of my notebooks. But something was different. These songs didn't sound anything like the Gospel music I'd grown up

with, or even the newfangled Gospel songs I'd been singing with PTL. I was finally realizing that I wanted to have
a career in music that wasn't focused on traditional Gospel
songs. I worried about the criticism and the pushback I'd
face from our audience and maybe from my own family.
People who had bought that first record by CeCe and me
could be completely uninterested in BeBe if he wasn't
singing that old Gospel music.

Ronald cut through all my meandering words during
this conversation. He looked me straight in the eyes and
told me what I'd been afraid to admit to myself. The
reason that I was wavering was that I wanted nothing
short of stardom. I'd been told my whole life that pride
was a terrible thing. I thought trying to become a celebrity
would only feed my pride.

Ronald joked that I'd wanted everyone's eyes on me
since I was a little lad. I winced through this part of the
conversation, but I was smiling too. I wanted to be big
and successful and internationally known. Ronald knew it,
CeCe knew it—maybe my parents even knew it! I was the
last to admit it to myself. Ronald encouraged me to get
comfortable with what I wanted. The rest of the Winanses
knew who I was. And they were still going to cheer for
me. I needed to start seeing my dreams in a different
way—in a way that didn't depict my ambition in such a
negative light. I could envision myself in a spotlight for
God's glory, no matter what I was singing.

CHAPTER EIGHTEEN

SAYING GOODBYE TO JIM AND TAMMY

"Men of Galilee," they said, "why do you stand here looking into the sky? This same Jesus, who has been taken from you into heaven, will come back in the same way you have seen him go into heaven."

—Acts 1:11

It was hard to tell Jim and Tammy that we were going to leave. They had truly become parents to us. My mother sent us down to Pineville as teens, and Jim and Tammy took on parent roles. In those early years of working and honing our gifts, we grew to be a family. The bonds were tight and real, no matter how awkward we felt with the other singers after we became successful.

But how do you tell someone you love so much that you're leaving? You're not only saying goodbye to your livelihood; you're saying goodbye to friends, to kin.

With Ronald's encouragement fresh in my mind, CeCe and I went to dinner at the Bakkers' house. I knew this was most likely the last dinner that we'd share with them. This time, I knew we would be able to tell them what was on our mind. Ronald had reminded me that my future was mine, not the Bakkers'. Though Jim and Tammy had made a place for us in Pineville, God had other things planned for us. Even the Bakkers couldn't stand in the way of that.

Dinner conversation began the way it normally did. The table at Jim and Tammy's end was buzzing with excitement and celebration. The Bakkers praised the quality of the service, of our singing, and lauded the success of the PTL mission. CeCe and I felt no obligation to join them. It was then that they knew that something was wrong, and a hush came over Jerusalem.

We still had trouble getting the words out.

"What's wrong, you two?" they asked us.

"Everything is fine. But we have something very difficult that we need to discuss with you."

Then we had to say the words we'd been trying to speak to them for the past few months.

"We feel like God is calling us to leave the PTL."

Their mouths fell open.

I continued, trying to be as gentle as I could.

"We've made our decision and can't be persuaded otherwise," I said.

We heaped gratitude on them again, thanking them for welcoming us and giving us a home. I told them that our decision was made with prayer. But the reaction was what you might have expected.

Tammy broke down completely, while Jim tried to comfort her.

"Why do you have to leave? We love you," Tammy cried.

I remember Tammy crying as she told us over and over again, "You're our children. You're our children!"

"We love you too," we replied.

I awkwardly tried to talk over her sobs, but it was pointless. Tammy was reacting like someone had died in front of her.

Jim explained they wanted us to stay while we focused on our rising duet stardom. Everything he said was true. We could still pursue what we were doing as part of the show. But sometimes you just know it is time to move on. And it was time.

Pain, I learned, is a part of life. This was a painful decision, especially because we were so deeply connected.

Then Jim said something I'll never forget. He said, "I'm not saying this because I'm trying to hold you here. But you and CeCe are going to become more famous than you know."

He spoke like a prophet to us. And I asked myself, "How in the world does he know this?" It seemed an incredible and insane thing to say to us since we were walking away from this great opportunity with PTL.

Jim's words also reminded me of the reality of my faith. How often do we say we have faith or that our faith will carry us through? And then, when the rubber hits the road, we're surprised at how difficult it is to live by our own words. Walking by faith and not by sight sounds great coming out of our mouth, but our legs are quick to remind us how hard those words can be to live out. Faith is blind. If you asked me tomorrow where I'm going from here, I would tell you I don't know. I only hope that I can summon up the strength to obey and to follow Him, to go where He leads.

It was a hard conversation to have with two friends we loved so much. But Jim and Tammy were gracious to us. Looking back, it shows how wonderful they really are. I've seen in the church world when a layperson or even a staff member might say, "God's moving me to another church," and the pastor responds with cynicism. We are too quick to be selfish with people. Even in the midst of Tammy crying, "Don't go," Jim was encouraging.

And that's been his MO since I've known him. I remember the day I received a phone call offering CeCe and me a star on the Hollywood Walk of Fame. That was a surreal phone call. And guess who my next phone call was to? Yes,

I called Jim, and he congratulated us. Jim Bakker. Thirty years earlier he told us we were going to be stars, and now there we were, getting a star on the Hollywood Walk of Fame. It was the first time a brother/sister duo received a star. Jim, the encouraging prophet and friend.

As a child, I was taught about walking through the door that God opened, but I didn't know that that door was going to be the door to the Bakkers' house. It was time to leave PTL behind and walk hand in hand with the Lord, into the contradictions that would make up my future. Gospel or R&B? Both?

I would never know unless I left. Looking back on it now, I wonder if I was ready to leave PTL. It was time, but was I prepared for the immense change that was about to take place in my life? I dreamed about heading out into the music scene, but in the same minute, I balked at the scope of the challenge. CeCe was less concerned, probably because she was in love with Mr. Love. Sometimes you just have to step into the next part of life without being ready. And so, we did.

Our farewell from PTL was tearful. Tammy kept crying. We cried too. We'd miss PTL, Jim, and Tammy.

I reminded myself that I'd be under a different light the next time I sang as the spotlight turned off. The curtains went down, and the audience applauded. I breathed a sigh of relief and sadness. Jim and Tammy gathered all the PTL Singers together to see us off after our final show. I could see smiles in the crowd of singers, but some people were genuinely sad. Some of them would be grateful to see us go. It would be an answer to their prayers. More of them would get those coveted solos now that CeCe and I would be out of the picture. (But soon after we left, more African American faces were added on their television network.)

To my surprise, some singers came around at the very end. I don't want to say they were gracious only because it's easy to be gracious when people are leaving. I think that our presence truly caused a change of heart in them. We were still viewed, largely, as Jim and Tammy's pet project, and many felt that our presence on PTL had been an act of charity and goodwill on the part of the Bakkers more than our genuine talent. Many couldn't admit that people of another race could be measured by the same bar of talent.

As I shook hands and took in smiles, I tried to tell who was sincere and who wasn't. I hoped that I'd been able to teach them something about acceptance since I had come so far from my Detroit home and had given so much of my time to PTL. As I looked around, for the last time, at the sea of white faces, something occurred to me. The job of teaching these people to accept me was bigger than I was and longer-standing than my time on PTL. They hadn't hated us because we had different skin color. These people had been taught that we were evil. Two kids, just trying to sing their hearts out to the Lord. Me, a boy trying to be a man. CeCe, a sweet and beautiful soul from the moment she was born. Evil? We were more like them than they'd ever know.

From the time that they were children, these Southern ladies and gentlemen had been told that they were better than we were. Staying away from us was not only a righteous thing to do, it was the safest thing to do. It was the only thing to do. It was an insidious lesson—the only way to keep yourself safe is to stay around people who look like you and think like you. Everybody else is dangerous and wants to hurt you.

I tried to place myself in their shoes then. They had to overcome these biases that had been sown in their hearts when they were vulnerable. They would have to work to reject the lessons of every parent, relative, Sunday school teacher, and classroom that they'd ever known. Understanding and loving people like CeCe and me would mean reexamining their entire experience.

I thanked the Lord that I had never been taught to hate.

CeCe and I waved goodbye to our PTL family, a family that had been as rife with drama and complications as the most contentious of families.

JIM AND TAMMY

Having received my first TV and recording experience at PTL, I've often been asked about Jim and Tammy. I can only tell my story, that Jim and Tammy Bakker were like parents to me and CeCe. They fostered our talent and our dreams. But like all parents, they made mistakes, had some grievous oversights, and had to face the consequences of their actions and errors.

But I want to be clear: Jim and Tammy didn't hurt us. Either of us—ever. I do not presume to speak for those who were hurt. Some will look at my story and say the Bakkers used us. Who can judge the whole heart but the Lord? But what I can tell you with absolute certainty is that they loved us.

CeCe and I propelled PTL to a kind of success that they couldn't match after we left. We brought something special, beautiful, and different to the show. The Winanses and the Bakkers came from truly different worlds. There were truths and nuances about the world that CeCe and I came from that the Bakkers could never understand. And vice versa. But they did welcome us into their world, broken though it may have been, and I do believe that they genuinely loved us.

Within just a few years, Pineville didn't resemble the Pineville I'd done some growing up in. Sadly, Jim and Tammy's empire fell apart completely. But even now I know that Jim learned so much through that difficult time. And some of that learning and wisdom he has imparted to me along the road of life. I still consider him a great friend and love him.

CHAPTER NINETEEN

NOT QUITE READY TO FLY

For I am convinced that neither death nor life, neither angels nor demons, neither the present nor the future, nor any powers, neither height nor depth, nor anything else in all creation, will be able to separate us from the love of God that is in Christ Jesus our Lord.

—Romans 8:38–39

We were blessed, we were confused, and we were headed back to Detroit. CeCe arrived first, and after a year living on my own in Charlotte, I decided to return to Detroit, as well.

Back in Detroit, I faced discord and hate of a different kind. All people are terribly contradictory—that's the

187

only thing I've found about people that remains the same. And all of us fight the contradictions in our lives. Some of us fight them until the end, and some of us learn to accept them. That's what I tried to do once I returned to Detroit.

My fears about our new style of music were not un-founded. I nervously waited for the reaction that our music would make in our neighborhood. The news was not good. Our new record, *Lord Lift Us Up,* had made the rounds, and the word got out after our performances. It might have been a vocal minority, but plenty of people were angry about the songs we were singing. These songs weren't Gospel, and, they complained, they weren't praising God either. They were outright blasphemy. I don't know what hurt the most, accusations coming from people I grew up singing with or from the people I didn't know at all.

You can absolutely believe these things upset Mom and the rest of the family. She couldn't believe that our community didn't rally around us and our success. One minute, our neighbors were complaining that white people were trying to keep black people from succeeding, and the next, they were furious at the particular kind of success that the Winans kids had achieved. I would soon really understand that the root of most of it was jealousy. Whatever it was, they were not as open and as accepting as Mom and Dad had been. Mom and Dad loved us, loved our music, and saw the way that it gave glory to God.

But sometimes people just aren't ready for a change. I don't think anybody's ready for change, including me. Change, I've learned, is a wonderful thing. But we become comfortable with where we live, who we hang out with, and what we do in life. Bills are paid. Life seems wonderful.

Then, all of a sudden, God says, "Time for change."

"Have you lost your mind, God? I'm not going any-where. Everything's good, and this is what I prayed for. And this is what you gave to me," we reply.

Suddenly we know more than our Heavenly Father? We know more than the one who created us? We don't desire change, but the lyrics to the song "Everything Must Change," by Benard Ighner, remind us that "everyone will change / no one stays the same." That's for sure. But an even greater certainty is this: God never changes, and He is faithful all the time.

CHAPTER TWENTY

HOW WHITNEY HOUSTON TAUGHT ME TO GUARD MY HEART

In grammar school some of the girls had problems with me. My face was too light. My hair was too long. It was the black-consciousness period, and I felt really bad. I finally faced the fact that it isn't a crime not having friends. Being alone means you have fewer problems. When I decided to be a singer, my mother warned me I'd be alone a lot. Basically we all are. Loneliness comes with life.

—Whitney Houston, interview in *TIME*,
1987

As I quickly found out, life doesn't get any less complicated with more fame. If anything, things become more complex and fuller of contradiction.

Let me take you back to a moment—a special night that brought a new light into my life.

In my life that I only wished was simple and straightforward, I was still a young man, and CeCe and I were getting some wider recognition for our music—recognition outside our Detroit community, which still couldn't figure out how they felt about us. I was a young man on the brink of stardom. And on that special night, I had walked down a red carpet while cameras flashed. I was wearing my Sunday best.

I couldn't believe we were sitting in L.A.'s Shrine Auditorium for an awards show. This was one of those moments that I had only been able to dream of, and it was actually happening. This was a grander auditorium than the Pineville studio—by a long shot. This whole event was much bigger than PTL. I stared around, and I felt as though I could recognize every face. I couldn't believe that I was actually one of these faces, that we had actually been nominated. If everything went according to my plan, we'd be saying thank you to all those famous faces in just a few moments.

I froze as the announcer read off the nominees' names, microphone in hand. I let myself believe, just for one moment, that we would actually win. Well, I can't really say that I had been rehearsing a victory speech for that night, but I can say that in my head for most of my adolescent life I knew one day I would win and then probably be speechless. Sitting there hoping for a positive outcome for me and my sister and then, well, boom. It felt like my heart dropped below my chair when the announcer read the winning names.

And they weren't ours.

I watched with heartbreak as the winners got up, shuffled past their seatmates, and walked down the aisle to the stage to the sound of tumultuous applause.

I thought about how I had let myself dip into the elation of the moment, only to have a taste. I felt myself blush. I tried to smile, but it must have been more of a grimace. I don't even want to know. Our record was good, and it had done very well. After months of hoping, doubting, and flustered excitement, we had lost.

I watched the rest of the ceremony with glazed eyes, clapping when I was supposed to and trying to smile. It was a relief when it was finally over. Coming to an awards show that you lose feels more like a slap in the face than an honor, and I was really letting that show. I hadn't done this particular dance before, and as I look back on it, I know I was overreacting. There would be more awards to win and lose in the future, and I would get much better at being gracious. But in that moment, I was a young man who felt like he had been humiliated in front of all his idols. I was angry, mostly at myself, and I was making a plan to make sure that next time we were here, we'd win, and I would accept the win with gratitude.

AN UNLIKELY VISITOR

In the wake of the loss, standing in the theater looking around, I heard a voice say, "Who are you looking for, big head?" And as I turned around to the direction of that voice, I saw that it was coming out of the woman who had become *the voice* that was wowing the world: Whitney Houston.

With a laugh I replied, "I'm looking for you, with your big head." We hugged, and then I introduced Whitney to CeCe. Somehow in that moment of lows, in that moment of losing the award, coupled with the highs of seeing Whitney again, that night broke through it all, and she asked, "What are you guys doing after the show?"

"Well, we're leaving now because we have two shows at a small venue in Redondo Beach. One starts at ten p.m. and the other at midnight."

To our surprise, Whitney said, "OK, I'm coming to the midnight show!" Without much thought, I said, "Shut up, girl. You're lying. You're not coming to our show at midnight."

But she insisted.

"I'll be there tonight!"

I gave her and Robyn, her assistant, the info, we hugged and said goodbye.

Now, let me be perfectly honest. There was just no way on earth we believed that this incredibly talented star was coming to see us at midnight on the same night of a hectic awards show. Just, no way. But to our delight and surprise, at 11:55 p.m., and I mean exactly 11:55 p.m., Whitney Houston walked into that small venue, and they brought her to our closet of a dressing room. She was all smiles, saying, and I quote, "I told y'all I was coming. Y'all thought I was lying. I *told* y'all I was coming."

And that was the day when strangers with admiration for each other became friends and family until what we know now was a bitter end. That night is something I will always be grateful for. Beyond the loss, we found a great friend who ended up on that small stage with CeCe and me, singing a song I wrote with a friend, Percy Bady, called, "Love Said Not So." The lyric that resounds in my head reminds me that "love told me love said not so," even with the odds against me. And yes, the odds that night at the awards and beyond have been against me, but what I learned about God is this: If God be for you, then who can be against you? God is love, and what He says about me is the most important thing anyone can say. And He told me that even with the odds against me, "not so."

Whitney Houston was the kind of star who made us look like local stars with little success. But right there, in our dressing room, she began to tell us how much she was a fan and how our music was a lifeline for her and that she knew all our songs. The moment immediately became surreal again.

The room inhaled her. And it held its breath while she stood in it. And I think I did too. Whitney loved life. She loved *living* life. I understand that now, after knowing her for most of my adult life. But in that moment, anyone would have noticed that about her. She was like a breeze off the summer shore. She brought refreshment and joy to the moment. And I'll never forget it.

Then she proceeded to blow my mind.

Whitney immediately cut through all the stardom stuff and treated us like family and demanded we do the same. She became our biggest fans. "Y'all family," she said. And we were.

That kind of attitude, that kind of nonchalance about her fame and celebrity, that's what was so special about Whitney. She just wanted to be Nippy—that's what her mother and close friends called her.

I can add all this color to this story now, but at the time, my brain was working overtime. I knew the moment was so much more than Whitney just wanting to be friends— at least to my young mind and heart. I privately resolved that our concert would have to be the best concert that we had ever performed. Resolving to be the best was a Winans family thing, so whenever we recorded a CD or performed live, we wanted it to be our best or face the family review.

In the immediate Winans clan, family can get competitive due to the talent pool and people vying to be the best. I'm sure we all inherited this from Skippy, our father. Maybe Mom can say for sure.

And remember, within the family there were several equations or formulations of Winanses. You had my brothers' group, the Winans; the duet BeBe & CeCe; my brother Daniel, who had now become a solo artist because of CeCe's and my departure; and with time other groups emerged from our household. But in the last part of the eighties and the beginning of the nineties, there was heated and healthy competition within the Winans family. You didn't want to follow a sibling's successful CD with the release of your own unsuccessful CD—no, no. That would give our family a platform for unwanted sarcasm that could end in a fight. And when it did, that's when Mom and Dad stepped in and reminded us of some very important truths: this was hard work since there were ten of us, and often, more than one or two of us was at fault in their eyes. They reminded us that jealousy had no place in our household, but most important, they reminded us of the definition of family and how we had to be there for one another and if one Winans wins, all Winanses win, and if one Winans loses, then all Winanses lose. My father assured us that God had a plan for each one of us and that we were there to promote God and help one another, and the gifts we shared were the gifts God had given our family.

Considering the line of preachers in my family—my great-grandfather, my grandfather, and my father—you can imagine how those powwows would be filled with Scripture on all sides. Yes, Winanses knew how to sing, but we also knew what you needed to bring to an argument— God's word. Quoting the Bible was one sure sign that we knew we had done something wrong. Eventually, the truth prevailed, and love and forgiveness were on display and normal life at the Winans residence continued as usual, loving God and one another with all our hearts.

CELEBRITY HAS ITS PRIVILEGES

When Whitney said she was family, she meant it—through thick and thin. She was committed to us. I remember once when Whitney agreed to sing on our new CD before even contacting or telling anyone at her record label, Arista, where Clive Davis ruled and reigned in a good way. When I shared that news with our record company, they were excited but doubtful it would happen because this was Whitney Houston—not some random background singer. Record companies are not in the business of sharing profits with other record companies. Yet due to some contractual complications, Whitney's attorney called and told me what our record company thought would happen.

"She loves you guys, but I'm sorry to tell you, Whitney can't sing on your record."

"That's disappointing, but we understand," I said to Whitney's attorney.

You can imagine Whitney's surprise when she called me up and asked how my talk with the attorney and record label went. Whitney was fully expecting to get things rolling.

"Well, there are some complications," I told her.

"Complications? What complications? Oh no," she said.

I tried to tell her it was OK and that we understood.

"Hang up the phone," she said, fuming.

I hung up.

I started to accept the facts. This was Whitney Houston. What were we thinking getting our hopes up? As if she'd ever be allowed to sing with the likes of us, this little Gospel duo from Detroit.

Then the phone rang.

It was Whitney's attorney.

"Uh-huh. OK. That's . . . great."

I hung up the phone.

Suddenly, everything was all cleared up. She could sing with us.

After she came to our concert, Whitney started campaigning for CeCe and me. Part of her plan to promote us was to sing on our next record. We were stunned. What kind of person, especially in her position, does that?

She was adamant about our success—a generous spirit I'll never forget.

Singing with her was like a miracle too. And I thought to myself that I wanted to be that kind of artist one day. The kind of artist who opens doors for other artists no matter what the label says or thinks.

She sang with us, we sang for her, and we always had a blast doing so. And she gave us all the music industry knowledge we needed. When she wasn't singing to millions of fans around the world, she flew to wherever we were and just came and hung out and laughed all night long. She was a star, an artist, a sensation—but she was our friend, and we loved her.

I didn't know then that a life such as Whitney's could be so complicated. Seeing it from afar, you don't see all the nuance of a person's life. You don't see what they must endure. But the closer you become to the person, the more you understand.

I remember the first time she invited us over to her house. When we arrived, we just hung out in her beautiful home, eating, laughing, and getting to know one another. Another time she invited us over just before CeCe and I were about to embark on our first headlining tour, which was a big feat for a Gospel artist. Later that evening she said, "Come on. Follow me." And she led us to one of her closets. Yes, she invited us into her closet. But it was no ordinary closet. It was about the size of my house. We sat in her closet talking about life, music, dreams, and then she showed us the set of costume designs she was having made for our upcoming tour. And not only outfits for us, but for our band and our backup singers! It totally caught us off guard.

It was in the intimate confines of her closet that she told us and then showed us how much we meant to her. After her little fashion show, we just sat there and laughed for hours. As time went on, she told us about how her fast rise to fame affected her; all she really wanted to be was herself again—that Whitney who enjoyed singing when there weren't cameras following her every move and people making up stories about her. She told us about the loneliness that comes with it all.

Some folks see the stars and say, "They should be thankful for all they have—how can you complain about the so-called trouble associated with fame? Be careful what you ask for."

Well, Whitney was not complaining to us. She understood how the business worked. But even so, one can never gauge the amount of exposure that comes with being someone like Whitney Houston. That kind of stardom affects everything, especially your personal life and the lives of your family and friends. Whitney loved to sing, and the most enjoyable time singing was when she was off the stage and in church, where she expressed the love she had for the One who loved her the most. Now, she was fierce when she had to be; she could hang with the best of them. But when she was around friends and family, she was a little sarcastic girl from the neighborhood with a heart of gold.

Those early years with Whitney seem like a dream now. I still can't believe she's gone. But I will not forget that night in her closet. And I'll also never forget what she taught me, just by being my friend. She helped me understand the reality that you must not listen to what people say about you, but to always guard your heart. That's the only way the effects of success don't overwhelm you.

In Proverbs 4:23, it says to "guard your heart, for everything you do flows from it." Now, Whitney was no preacher—though she could bring down a church with her anointed lungs—but she knew truth. And knowing the importance of guarding your heart? That's truth.

Success in this life, and I mean any kind of success, not just the kind that awards you with Grammys, can invite all kinds of people and thoughts and things into your life that shouldn't be there. Success, if not kept in check, can grow pride to a size that's impossible to control. It can poison your faith with skepticism. It can poison your hope with despair. And it can poison your love with hate. So be on your guard. Don't let success rule you and steal your life. Keep your heart strong.

Keep it strong with time spent with friends and loved ones.

Keep it strong with the nurturing water of forgiveness.

Keep it strong with the mysterious power of beauty.

Keep it strong by chasing your dreams even when it seems as though they're unreachable.

Keep it strong by resisting pride.

Keep it strong by staying generous.

Keep it strong by never forgetting who you are or where you came from.

My heart was like an open barn door flapping in a storm when I was younger. And I didn't learn much of this list in those early years. But it was real people, true people, like Whitney who helped mold my heart into something I'd learn to protect.

CHAPTER TWENTY-ONE

HOW MUCH DOES
MY SOUL COST?

Not everybody can be famous, but everybody can be great, because greatness is determined by service.

—Martin Luther King Jr.

As we became more famous, I started wondering if I had taken a wrong step somewhere. Yes, the concerts and the records were what I had always wanted, but sometimes we want things that aren't good for us. I didn't want to gain the whole world at the cost of my own soul. Did God really want me to pursue success like this? Was I still singing to make His name famous instead of my own? With that caution, I decided to retrace my steps.

One day, around 1984, after we had been away from PTL

for a year or so, the phone rang at my home in Detroit, and it was a familiar voice from Pineville. This person made a request on behalf of Jim and Tammy Bakker: please come back to PTL. I was caught off guard. But I had to ask myself, "Is this the answer to my question?" The next phone call was to CeCe. And after long talks and prayer, we both decided and agreed to go back to Charlotte. We would still be able to continue building our careers as a duo outside of the network while still being a part of PTL.

All things pointed to Charlotte as a solid home base for CeCe and me again. With our careers on the upswing and feeling good about our decision to return to PTL, the phone rang again. With only weeks before CeCe and I would be leaving our homes in Detroit, the unexpected happened. The same person who called to share the request from Jim and Tammy for us to come back to Charlotte delivered the news that Jim had changed his mind. The offer was withdrawn. Just like that, with no other explanation. Goodbye.

We wondered what was going on. A week later we watched the news and, along with the rest of the world, witnessed the fall of Jim and Tammy and the PTL Network's whole empire.

It was shocking and painful to watch people criticize Jim and Tammy. People Jim and Tammy had helped turned on them. People who once called Jim and Tammy their brother and sister in Christ were now calling them a cancer in the body of Christ—a cancer that needed to be cut out. I was stunned and overwhelmed with emotion. The betrayal was astonishing to me. From friends to enemies in the blink of an eye.

I experienced a lot of "You aren't Christian enough," or "You're too Christian. "Is your music Gospel or R&B?" or "Are you from Detroit or Hollywood, and no, it can't be both!" But my attempt to empathize felt pretty empty. Jim and Tammy were suffering much more than we had when it came to cruel words. Some I'd read in the papers were surprising but also intensely mean. And I knew we were much more stalwart than Tammy. I couldn't imagine the effect that the PTL problems were having on Tammy's view of herself. I knew her heart must have been under tremendous strain.

What did I do for my friends in that moment?

I prayed and cried and prayed some more for those two people who had been nothing but good to me. Sure, they might have made some mistakes in how they loved us when we were on the show, but I knew their hearts. I knew they cared and intended good. As I prayed and cried for them, I thought of my years on the show and all that I learned and experienced. It was good to reminisce. Together we had changed so many hearts, and that work was more meaningful than any number of record sales.

What hurt the most was not being able to help keep Jim

and Tammy from the awful pain the world was serving. Truth mixed with untruth is unfair.

The withdrawn invitation started to make sense. Jim knew their world was about to crumble, and he didn't want his African American children to be caught up in that web. He was protecting us just like a father does his children.

It was hard for us to watch, knowing our hurt was nothing like Jim and Tammy and their family's hurt. I'm still shocked at how much they endured during that time—the constant attacks and betrayals were crushing. I prayed for them constantly, asking God to show mercy and grace. After Jim was sent to prison, our relationship was null and void.

We are still His children, when we're right and when we're wrong. The Bible often reminds us of His unfailing love. I believe that God is still married to the backslider and that mercy and grace follow us for all the days we have on planet Earth, even when we're feeling helpless and vulnerable. No one likes that feeling—when the world stares down at you when once they looked up to you and wanted to hear what you had to say.

There were days I wondered if we could have helped by showing with our presence how these two people had hearts for the Lord and His children who were hurting around the world.

CHAPTER TWENTY-TWO

LOVE & FREEDOM

But seek first his kingdom and his righteousness,
and all these things will be given to you as well.

—Matthew 6:33

Time hopscotches, and with time came gold records and now, a platinum album. Through all the accolades and the awards, before my brother Ronald went home to be with Jesus, he was always there to cheer us on.

He was proud of his baby brother and sister, and the other siblings too. He made many sacrifices to be present in our lives in Charlotte and beyond, every moment he could.

Ronald always understood so much. He knew that PTL remained a sweet spot in my heart and represented a place that was familiar and safe.

Every musician's biggest dream is a gold and platinum record! But with that I had my doubts because the future is unknown. It's scary when you're not in control of tomorrow. What would happen in this new unknown world—this new path that seemed to be the only possible way forward? The world of platinum albums was a scary place. In an instant, everything could go so terribly wrong. What if the same kind of tragedy that had befallen Jim and Tammy happened to us? Everything felt so tenuous. But even worse, I had discovered that fame and success wouldn't shield me from being hurt and brought low by other people. That kind of protection didn't exist.

Thank goodness Ronald was wise. He told me to stay steady, to keep the faith, and God would reveal His will for my life.

Ronald seemed to always have a good word at just the right time. He just always reminded of God's promises, even the promises I wrote about in my songs. That was a very Winans kind of thing we'd say to one another too. We needed to listen to the words that we were singing. And we needed to *hear* them and heed them. And even though people told me that my music was the Devil's music, the lyrics were still about God's love for us and the way that He brings redemption to all our low places. Always thanking those who spoke wisdom into my life and resolved to keep my heart into my music, no matter how many times I was hurt. And if it turned one person's thoughts to heaven, then that was enough. And that includes me.

Our music and our talent had started back in Detroit, been fostered in Pineville, and now it was something completely our own.

Even with a platinum record hanging on the wall and a closed door marked "PTL" behind us, our future was wide open, and I had no idea where we were going to go. I rolled up my sleeves and said yes to the one who can do beyond all we can ask or think. And all I had to do was ask and believe.

CHAPTER TWENTY-THREE

THE FAME THAT MATTERS MOST

Perhaps home is not a place but simply an irrevocable condition.

—James Baldwin, *Giovanni's Room*

I will never forget the day we lost Ronald.

It was like Ronald was putting his arms around me and whispering one last piece of wisdom into my ears. My name might be on record labels and up in lights. But that didn't matter. There was only one place that my name needed to be, and that was in God's book of life. My name could be inscribed on one of those Grammy Awards, but it wouldn't mean anything. It could be on the lips of millions of people, all praising my music, but that wouldn't mean anything either.

We live in a world that clamors for the applause of the crowd. The sound of applause is gratifying, and it can be addicting. Once we get it, it's hard to live without it. I've heard stories about professional football players who say how hard it is to give up the game because it brings so much satisfaction, and along with the thrill of the crowd and the lights and the big game atmosphere, it's a hard thing to live without.

That yearning for stardom, that longing to be in the spotlight, that was all well and good, but absolutely none if it would matter if my name wasn't in the right book— the only book, God's book. Being in God's book is about being famous with God and understanding that He loves me and that He thinks I'm great no matter what kind of style of music I'm singing, no matter what mistakes I've made or will make.

I looked at Ronald's body lying in the bed. His name had been inscribed in the right book. And I wanted mine to be there too—I wanted all of us to be in that book together, and the worldly recognition could take a distant second place.

Through tears, I nodded over at Ronald. I'd make sure I remembered that my name was already known to the only one who mattered. And someday, I knew that I'd see Ronald again in the only home that we'd ever really belong to.

When I was a young boy, I sensed in my heart what I wanted to do in life. It was literally in my blood. I was nourished in a home built, and focused, on music. I wanted to be great. Sunday never came soon enough. When you know you are born to do something, you do it regardless of any kind of success or fame or financial reward that might be attached to it. My brother Ronald reminded me all the time that yes, I was a Winans, but also a child of God. I was created in His likeness. It was God's grace that reminded me to not only sing the lyrics that I wrote but to live the lyrics as well. In essence, grace reminded me to sing and keep singing regardless of what anyone said, regardless of the accolades, and regardless of the criticisms.

When I think back over my story, and the obstacles, the disappointments, the victories, the surprises, the racism, and the love, I'm convinced that if you and I can live like we understand our value before God, if you and I can live knowing our neighbor's value before God, then we can participate in a daily glory and peace for which we were all born.

ACKNOWLEDGMENTS

I want to acknowledge first my Friend, my Hope, and my Lord Jesus Christ for loving me the way no one else could and for giving me something no one else would—His Life. I thank you with my life.

To my Winans family, David, Ronald, Carvin, Pastor Marvin, Michael, Daniel, Cece, Angie, and Debbie: I love you like family should—and that is unconditionally!!

To my offspring, Miya and Benjamin: you are the gifts that keep on giving. And, yes, gifts come with a price and a price tag. LOL!

To my mom, Delores Amelia Winans: I say you and I make a great team!!! And I wouldn't trade you for nothing. I love you maybe too much.

To Tim Willard: It's again an honor to work beside you.

Your talent is gigantic, and your heart and passion are equal to your talent. Thanks again for the ride.

To Jan Miller Rich and the team at Dupree Miller & Associates: Thank you for your guidance and your commitment to further my voice to the world. I wouldn't want to do it without you. Jan, on a personal note, thanks for being family—you and Jeff mean the world to me. Love you guys.

To Rolf Zettersten and the FaithWords team at Hachette Book Group: Thank you for your faith in me and my story. It's been a long journey, and I'm glad to share this part with you.

Special thanks to those in my inner circle who have surrounded me and challenged me for many years. Ron Gillyard, my brother and friend, let's just continue to do what some say is impossible.

My steadfast friends Margaret Bell (the best), Harry Dawkins (next to the best), and many others I could name...but it would take up too much paper. Love you all!

DISCOGRAPHY

SOLO ALBUMS

1997: *BeBe Winans* (Atlantic)

2000: *Love & Freedom* (Motown)

2002: *Live and Up Close* (Motown)

2004: *My Christmas Prayer* (The Movement Group / Hidden Beach / Epic)

2005: *Dream* (The Movement Group / Still Waters / Hidden Beach)

2007: *Cherch* (The Movement Group / Koch)

2012: *America America* (My Destiny / Razor & Tie)

AS BEBE & CECE WINANS

1984: *Lord Lift Us Up* (PTL)
1987: *BeBe & CeCe Winans* (Sparrow / Capitol)
1988: *Heaven* (Sparrow / Capitol)
1991: *Different Lifestyles* (Sparrow / Capitol)
1993: *First Christmas* (Sparrow / Capitol)
1994: *Relationships* (Sparrow / Capitol)
1996: *Greatest Hits* (Sparrow / EMI)
2006: *The Best of BeBe and CeCe* (Sparrow)
2009: *Still* (B&C / Malaco)

SINGLES

1996: "All of Me" (Myrrh)
1997: "In Harm's Way" (Atlantic)
1997: "Thank You" (Atlantic)
1997: "I Wanna Be the Only One" (with Eternal) (EMI)
1997: "Stay" (Atlantic)
2000: "Coming Back Home" (Motown)
2000: "Jesus Children of America" (Motown)
2000: "Tonight Tonight" (Motown)
2002: "Do You Know Him" (Motown)
2005: "I Have a Dream" (TMG / Still Waters)
2005: "Safe from Harm" (TMG / Still Waters)
2005: "Love Me Anyway" (TMG / Still Waters)
2018: "He Promised Me" (Malaco)
2018: "Laughter" (Malaco)

NOTES

1. The term "The Great Migration" is taken from the Pulitzer Prize–winning book *The Warmth of Other Suns* by Isabel Wilkerson. She wrote that the migration took place between 1915 and 1970: "Over the course of six decades, some six million black southerners left the land of their forefathers and fanned out across the country for an uncertain existence in nearly every other corner of America. The Great Migration would become a turning point in history." My brother Marvin, my co-writer, and I have discussed this time period as it relates to my great-grandfather I.W.

Winans and his decision to leave Mississippi and go north to Detroit to start a church. He felt compelled by God to do so. See Isabel Wilkerson, *The Warmth of Other Suns: The Epic Story of America's Great Migration,* (New York: Vintage Books, 2011), 1, 9.

2. This chapter is a compilation of a long conversation my collaborator and I had with my brother Marvin. In our conversation, Marvin told us the story of how he uncovered some new information on the family name when he went digging past I.W. Winans, our great-grandfather. I.W.'s father was Antonio Winans, but after Antonio, there is no record of names, just numbers—numbers we presume to be slave numbers. But we don't really know. After our conversation with Marvin, we contacted Millsaps College to get more information on Antonio Winans and the other Winanses who lived in the same area as Antonio and I.W. His name was William Winans, and he was a white Methodist itinerate preacher. We took our conversation with Marvin and filled in some of the holes by reading through the only biography written on

William Winans. It is a loose compilation of his life taken directly from his personal journals, letters, and sermons. We'll continue to explore the connection. For more on William Winans, see Ray Holder, *William Winans: Methodist Leader in Antebellum Mississippi* (Jackson: University Press of Mississippi, 1977).

3. Ibid., 23–25.

4. Ibid., 43. The biographer Ray Holder writes, "As Winans observed, bigotry and hostility tended to disappear 'when brought into intimate association with a natural state of society.'"

5. Ibid. See Chapter Four, "Squire of Rural Retreat."

6. Ibid., 45.

7. Ibid., 105–07.

8. I am indebted to Debra McIntosh, College Archivist at the Millsaps-Wilson Library of Millsaps College in Jackson, Mississippi. Debra was kind enough to forward me and my collaborator the archival list of William Winans. The bill of sale for a slave and the receipt of bequest of female negro are listed in Box 11.

9. See Laurent Dubois, "Introduction," in *The Banjo:*

America's African Instrument (Cambridge, MA: Belknap Press, 2016). See also "The Banjo's African American Heritage," African American Registry, accessed November 27, 2018, https://aaregistry.org/story/the -banjos-african-american-heritage.

10. "African American Song," Library of Congress, accessed November 27, 2018, https://www.loc.gov /item/ihas.200197451.

11. "Draft of Chapter IV, 'Love in Action,'" Martin Luther King, Jr., Research and Education Institute, accessed November 27, 2018, https://kinginstitute.stanford.edu /king-papers/documents/draft-Chapter-iv-love-action.

ABOUT THE AUTHOR

BeBe Winans is a six-time Grammy Award–winning artist and producer and host of his own radio show, *The BeBe Experience,* on the SiriusXM Radio channel Heart & Soul. Known for being among the first Christian singers to cross over into the mainstream and for his jaw-dropping performances, both solo and alongside his sister CeCe, BeBe has frequently appeared on national television— from *The Arsenio Hall Show* to *Good Morning America* to *The Oprah Winfrey Show*—and has acted in major motion pictures and Broadway productions.

For more information: BeBeWinans.net
Facebook, Instagram, Twitter: @BeBeWinans
Management & Booking: My Destiny Productions
mydestinyBW@gmail.com

VISIT US **BORNFORTHISBROADWAY**.COM

BORN

A NEW
MUSICAL

FOR THIS

ORIGINAL MUSIC & LYRICS   BOOK BY
BEBE   **CHARLES**   **BEBE**   **LISA**   CHOREOGRAPHER   DIRECTOR
WINANS   **RANDOLPH-WRIGHT, WINANS, & D'AMOUR**   **WARREN**   **CHARLES**
                                                                              ADAMS   **RANDOLPH-WRIGHT**

FOLLOW US